D0793505

Major Anders Lindgren's

TEACHING EXERCISES

A Manual for Instructors and Riders

Photo courtesy of United States
Dressage Federation, Inc.

Major Anders Lindgren's

TEACHING EXERCISES

A Manual for Instructors and Riders

Half Halt Press, Inc.
Boonsboro, Maryland

Major Anders Lindgren's

TEACHING EXERCISES
a Manual for Instructors & Riders

©1998 Major Anders Lindgren

Published in the United States of America by
Half Halt Press, Inc.
P.O. Box 67
Boonsboro, MD 21713

Book and jacket design by Design Point.

Printed in the United States of America

Library of Congress Cataloging-in-Publication Data

Lindgren, Anders.
    [Teaching exercises]
    Major Anders Lindgren's teaching exercises : a manual for
    instructors and riders.
        p.   cm.
    ISBN 0-939481-53-7
    1. Horsemanship--Study and Teaching. 2. Horsemanship.
I. Title. II. Title: Teaching exercises.
SF310.5. L55   1998
798.2'3--dc21   98-31462
                                                CIP

TABLE OF CONTENTS

FOREWORD

In 1979 I was invited to be the Head Teacher at the USDF/Vi Hopkins National Dressage Seminar. It was indeed an exciting time for me to go to the United States and start a National Seminar with ten mounted participating instructors and about 40 auditors. The first two years, I had the able assistance of two trainers from Denmark, Gunnar Ostergaard and Joergen Olsen.

I was already acquainted with Major Anders Lindgren from the sixties as a very good rider, 1971 Swedish Champion, 1972 Olympic competitor in Munich, and as a I judge and well-respected teacher at the Swedish Army Equestrian Center at Stroemsholm.

Major Lindgren was on my mind when in 1980 I looked for an assistant teacher for the 1981 USDF/Vi Hopkins Seminar. I personally considered him to be "the right man" to develop dressage in the U.S. I was aware he had retired from the Swedish Cavalry in 1975 and had begun his civilian career as an equestrian trainer in Sweden, Finland and Norway. I knew he had moved to southern Sweden, but I had difficulty finding him.

We finally crossed paths in November 1980 at The National Stud at Flyinge and I said to him, "I need your help! I have conducted two National Seminars at Tristan Oaks in Michigan in a program begun by Ms. Violet Hopkins in 1979. I need your help both as an assistant teacher and in developing the format. Would you come?" He immediately answered, "Thank you, Sir—I will come!"

So, in 1981 the USDF invited Major Lindgren to be my co-teacher and he was, right from the beginning, very popular. We had never met such an eager enthusiasm to learn before.

We had a different approach when teaching. His teaching method using the red traffic cones was something new and effective and the word was soon spread about "the Swede with the cones." The participants began to take notes on Major Lindgren's exercises and asked him to write a book.

Major Lindgren was again invited to the U.S. and has conducted nine National Seminars, four National Symposia, about 50 Regional Seminars and hundreds of clinics. He has been a very busy Major for nearly 16 years!

Now that he has shared his long teaching experience and his successful exercises in this book, I strongly recommend it for diligent study!

Aage Sommer
Hoersholm, Denmark
June 1998

Retired Colonel, Danish Cavalry, Olympic Judge, Head Teacher USDF/Vi Hopkins Seminar 1979-88

INTRODUCTION

"As for a long time I have occupied myself

with riding, I think I have accumulated some

experience with regard to the art of riding,

which makes it possible for me to elaborate on

the best way to treat horses in particular for the

benefit of the younger ones of my friends."

—Robichon de la Guérinière
1688-1751, Author of
Ecole de Cavalerie

In the same spirit as the great French riding master, I, too, believe I have accumulated some experience with regard to the art of riding, which I think makes it possible for me to write this book.

I have always been very interested in pedagogic. For 10 of my 30 years in the army, I served as a teacher at the Army Equestrian Center, for five years as Driving Master and for five years as Jumping Master. Also during my military service, I was a student at the Equestrian Center for two years, a platoon commander and then a company commander, and later a teacher at the Cavalry Cadet School as well.

Having been a competitor in each equestrian discipline at the national team level has helped me a great deal to understand the different problems and difficulties at hand, as well as giving me the knowledge and experience to help to solve them. My experience in driving has been especially valuable when teaching long reining to create obedience and collection.

In 1976 I was kicked by a horse and my arm was severely broken. It took a very good hand surgeon many hours to put the parts back together, followed by two more operations over the next year and a half. This was a very frustrating time for me because my arm was in a cast. I learned to do a lot of things using only my left hand and arm, but I could not ride.

I continued training students and their horses, but not always with as good a result as I wanted because I was unable to mount a horse and demonstrate an exercise and explain the aids from horseback. It was very frustrating when I was unable to ride a student's horse in order to help both the student and the horse to understand and improve. I consider it to be a teacher's duty to—now and then—mount a student's horse to learn if the training proceeds correctly.

It was especially difficult to get my students to understand and to ride precise school figures. One day, in frustration, I put some buckets upside down in the corner, and on the center line at X, two jump standards, which resembled the pillars in the manege at the Spanish Riding School in Vienna. It worked very well—my students started to navigate! They got their heads up and started to prepare their horses for corners, turns and circles. Later I bought and began to use smaller red traffic cones, which I kept in my car and brought with me to the different riding establishments where I was teaching.

I developed a system using the cones for less experienced riders, for young horses, and for my more advanced students and their trained horses as well. When introducing a new exercise, the placement of the cones made the new pattern clear to both the rider and the horse and the training became more successful.

The idea has been to explain my way of teaching throughout the levels with what are really lesson plans, along with comments and drawings for clarification. An Equestrian Cookbook of Equestrian Recipes! I hope it will be valuable for every instructor and for every rider—professional or amateur—in their daily work with horses and students.

This is the reason I have been so bold as to put all the exercises together for publication. The exercises here are arranged in the same order as the AHSA dressage tests, and at each level they are presented in sequences to carefully and gradually increase the difficulties in the training of the exercises. I hope they will help you.

I have had wonderful support from many friends to realize this book. First of all, however, I would like to thank my wife Puci for her brilliant ideas and her unceasing energy, encouragement, and interest in getting it done. I would like to thank Professor Janet Ver Plank for her advice as an author herself, Mrs. Vicki Matisi for her help with the original concept for the layout, Ms. Lena Acking for her realization of all the complicated drawings, Ms. Kathy Malone for her generous and invaluable advice and efforts to get this book published, Ms. Elizabeth Carnes, my publisher for a very pleasant cooperation and last, but not least, Ms. Christiane Noelting, who as a professional Instructor and Grand Prix Dressage rider has spent a lot of her expensive time to critically read the manuscript many times and she also completed some of the drawings.

Thank you all!

STATEMENTS, RULES OF THUMB AND GENERAL ADVICE

Navigare necesse est. One of the first sentences I learned in Latin. The translation is, "It is necessary to navigate!" For jumpers and eventers, this is very obvious: they must look for the next fence. For dressage riders, it is not so obvious. This is why the use of the small red cones in the arena helps teach them to navigate — to steer and control the course — and to choose focal points. If the rider — early and in advance — decides where to go, the horse will then go there!

Festina Lente. Another Latin sentence, this one meaning " Hurry slowly!" Here's another:

T. T. T. : Mind these three! Listen to their chime: "things take time" (or, think! take time!) — something to always consider and remember, when you train horses.

When Art Ends, Violence Begins. This sentence is written on the frame of the big mirror in the indoor arena at the Swedish Equestrian Center, at Stroemsholm. It is indeed a good reminder, when you face problems. A few words of advice: go to a more simple exercise.

The correct seat is the basic prerequisite for the applications of all aids.

The weight aids are the most essential and most influential ones, but also the most subtle and least noticeable. They are of particular importance as the rider's legs can only create the necessary impulsion when supported by the weight

The author on his pony "Mona" in 1935.

aid. The weight aid, the forward driving aids, the supporting legs, and the forward-sideways-driving leg aids instruct the horse what to do!

The reins are primarily of a regulating and explaining nature. They must always be accompanied by forward driving aids. The use of the reins must always be prepared by forward driving aids.

The Forward Driving Aids, Applied Step-By-Step:

▲ *Step 1.* Lift your chin. Tighten your shoulder blades. Inhale. Pinch your pelvis area forward using your abdominal power originating from solar plexus (the rectus abdominum).

▲ *Step 2.* **If the horse does not react:** Exhale and repeat Step 1, closing the vise of your legs around the horse's rib cage.

▲ *Step 3.* **If the horse still does not react** (as in "*Nobody home!*"): Exhale and repeat Steps 1 and 2, and use your calf and spurs to get attention. Punch the rib cage close behind the girth. Lower legs in a forward position means *forward*.

▲ *Step 4.* **If still nothing happens:** Exhale and repeat Steps 1, 2 and 3, and use your whip decisively. By using this kind of "consequent" education of the horse right from the very beginning, the aids become less and less noticeable until finally the rider seems to control the horse with only his thoughts and without any visible aids.

The rider's hand and the wrist have together 33 joints. When using the reins, the wrist joints must be supple. A useful comparison: flexibility like a rubber ring on a side rein.

The finger joints and the wrist must work with flexibility and step by step:

▲ *Step 1.* Squeeze the actual rein (like squeezing a piece of lemon). Every positive reaction is followed by a yielding of the rein—the *spontaneous reward*—that is, the release of the squeezing, prepared to repeat.

▲ *Step 2.* More regulating influence is given, when the rider repeats Step 1 and at the same time angles his wrist. He turns his little finger toward his belly button—like eating grapefruit with a spoon or eating yogurt with a spoon out of a mug. When turning the wrist the two bones in the lower arm, the ulna and the radius, are rotating around each other. A wonderful invention! At resistance, release the aids and repeat Steps 1 and 2.

▲ *Step 3.* **If the horse still resists:** Repeat Steps 1 and 2, and now — if necessary— the rider for the first time uses his elbow and shoulder joint. But, the horse never responds correctly to the rein aids **before the forward driving aids are accepted.** The horse must be in front of the riders legs!

A stern warning here: Never "get stuck in the horse's mouth;" that is, never end up pulling or hanging on the reins. A prolonged pull on the reins would only invite the horse to lean against the bit rather than obey the rein aid. The rider's hands, wrists and arms must work with sensitivity and flexibility, like "octopus arms," with light, sensitive and steady contact.

The Contact

Through contact with the horse's mouth through the reins, the rider learns to read the horse's mind. He learns to feel if the horse is accepting the bit with a desire to move or if the horse is behind the rider's legs.

The rider sits like a pilot in a cockpit of an aircraft with two jet engines in the rear end.

On the horse's back, though, the rider has no dash board with instruments. He cannot read the horse's "revolutions per minute" in the hind legs—the propulsion, so to speak—on an instrument. He must, through the rein contact, learn that a **strong contact, usually on the left rein** (the left hind leg—the left engine) works well.

If there is a weak, floppy contact, or no contact at all, on the right rein, the horse is not accepting the bit. The right hind — the right engine — does not work.

A Conclusion

If the mane falls to the right, which is normal, the horse's right side is usually the weak side. The left side is strong. The mane falls to the right because the more developed musculature on the strong side displaces the mane to the side where lesser development lets it fall over. If the mane falls to the left, which is the case among 25% of the horse population, the situation is the opposite—the left side is weak. The right side is strong.

What is better? To try to increase activity and power in the weak hind, or to decrease the power in the well-working hind leg?

Very often, riders think only of "stiff" and "hollow" sides of the horse. Irritated with the horse's heavier rein contact on his strong left side, they try to make it lighter through repeated work with the left hand and arm. They work in vain, and only increase the horse's ability to resist and increase his muscle power in the whole neck.

The Hammer and the Anvil

Listening to an instructor, you often hear, "Inside leg! Outside rein!" Most of the time, this is a correct instruction, but **rarely** do you hear an explanation of how and why.

Think of this: when a farrier bends a horse shoe, he must put it against an anvil before hammering. To teach riders to **apply** the outside leg as an anvil before using the inside leg usually requires a long period of patient instruction and work. It takes a long, long time before riders can effectively use their "anvil" to keep the horse in lateral balance and to redirect the energy created by the inner leg forward into the outside rein. Riders must learn to support the horse with their anvil (outside leg behind the girth) before applying their hammer (inside leg).

The Outside Rein

The outside rein is of regulating and controlling nature. It is necessary to explain very carefully and frequently the communication between the outside and the inside rein.

The instructor must explain how the outside rein:

1. **allows** the inside position (flexing) at the poll;

2. **allows** the horse (when and how) to turn;

3. **prevents** the horse from collapsing at the base of his neck when asked for the inside position of the poll;

4. **prevents** the horse from "popping" and falling over his outside shoulder.

Shuttling the Bit

Often a tense and nervous horse seems to be very stiff in the mouth. In this situation, the horse blocks the **atlanto-axis** joint (the joint at the poll between the first vertebra **atlas** (C 1) and the second **axis** (C 2), generally called the **axis joint.** When asked to flex his head either to the right or the left, the horse seems to say "No!"

When the horse relaxes in the **axis joint**, he normally begins listening to the riders aids.

To create this relaxation, the rider *shuttles* the bit in the horses mouth. To *shuttle* the bit means to move it through the horse's mouth like you move a shuttle through the loom when weaving. This should be a harmonious use of the reins in order to make the horse's mouth loose and mellow.

The rider should have a feeling of lubricating the **axis joint** with anti-rust oil.

Longitudinal Flexibility

Here, the horse's head is hanging on the first vertebra in the neck, the **atlas** (C 1). When the horse responds the rider's longitudinal influence with the reins, he relaxes in the area under the neck and in the jaws.

When yielding to longitudinal flexibility the horse seems to say, "Yes!"

Shuttling **the Bit and**
Creation of Longitudinal Flexibility

When the rider combines the management of the reins to achieve both the lateral and the longitudinal light contact, the horse learns to accept the bit. **It has nothing to do with an obvious cranking of the whole neck or see-sawing.**

This demands sensitivity, which comes naturally to some riders. Others must train and learn this sensitivity, preferably from riding well-trained horses, that is, schoolmasters.

This action is similar to the handling of the handle bar on a bicycle or the power steering wheel in a car.

But, remember, the horse never accepts the rein aids before the forward driving aids are accepted. **The horse must be in front of the rider's legs!**

 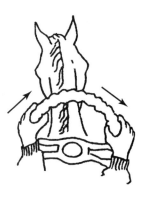

My advice: Train the student on the ground. Let him hold a bridle head with one hand and the bit in the other hand, and feel the different steps of rein management. Later let him practice the rein management while the instructor holds the bridle.

Remember: **The seven cervical vertebrae in the horse's neck should be as flexible as an elephant's trunk.**

The Half Halt (the Half-Parade)

Most European languages use the expression *half-parade,* instead of half-halt. **Parade** comes from the verb *parry*. In the sport of fencing, you *parry off* a thrust from a combatant by maneuvering your sword with short motions within your wrist alone, not by slashing with your whole arm like a pirate.

The command for a downward transition from trot to walk is, as translated from the German language," Please, parry your horse down to walk!"

The term *half halt* can give the rider the impression of using mainly the reins. But the term *half-parade* influences the rider to a more careful use of the forward pushing aids, combined with the parrying, non-pulling, management of the reins.

The half halt is used for the following purposes:

1. to prepare for downward transitions;

2. to slow down the pace;

3. to improve collection or shape of the horse within a pace;

4. to alert the horse before a new movement;

5. to regain a horse's correct shape;

6. to stop the horse leaning on the bit or rushing.

My Advice

To be successful, combine the aids for the half halt with the aids for a lateral movement such as leg-yielding, shoulder-fore or shoulder-in. Displace the horse's center of gravity laterally for a step or two and he is vulnerable to shifting his weight to the rear—in other words, to letting the half halt **go through.**

Downward Transitions

A downward transition is very similar to the descent with an aircraft towards the operating runway: the pilot has to fly in to the *touch down.*

Through the forward pushing aids combined with use of the non-allowing parrying reins, the rider enables the horse to bend the joints in the hind legs in order to switch his weight backwards for a *"touch down.*

Transitions

In every transition, the rider should encourage the horse to bend the joints in his quarters, to become more energetic behind, and to shift his weight back to at least horizontal level. That is, he horse accepts the half-parades.

These are, indeed, very severe demands, especially when riding young horses. However, by combining the aids for up or down transition with the aids for lateral movements such as leg-yielding, shoulder-fore or shoulder-in, the rider is able to displace the horse's center of gravity at the forehand. This is one effective way to teach the rider to get the horse in front of his legs in combination with the parrying reins. When the horse's center of gravity is disturbed, he reacts to try to rebalance his body. It means that he spontaneously increases his activity in the hind legs. In that situation he is more sensitive for the rider's aids and especially the reins. A comparison is when a person stumbles and starts to lose his

balance, he immediately starts to use his arms to be able to regain
balance and to protect himself from injuries if falling.

This need to displace the center of gravity at the shoulders, by the way, is why I teach my students to make leg-yielding with their inner driving leg **at**, not behind the girth.

Spooky Horses

My first advice: "Do not involve yourself in the horse's problem!"

Second advice: "Let your horse look at the suspicious spot!"

Third advice: "Look to the opposite side of the problem object, and ride the horse forward and away from the suspicious spot with the leg on when close to the spot. After some laps of the arena, the horse will begin to obey as the rider thinks and rides forward and does not care about the horse's problem."

Fourth advice: "Avoid pushing the horse closer toward a suspicious spot; this normally creates resistance and the horse learns to know about his physical strength, something he never is supposed learn."

Patterns: Why and How

Here is my philosophy of pattern use:

1. To use the figures, especially combined in a sequence.

2. To produce a gymnastic effect in the horse without requiring that the rider also be well-schooled. A correctly executed pattern schools the horse.

3. It is the choice of exercises and their sequence that produces the desired effect.

4. The rider learns by doing.

The Advantages

1. When the rider knows the pattern, the instructor does not need to give constant ring directions.

2. The instructor can, instead, give feedback as to how the exercise is being performed, or he can be quiet and allow his student to assimilate the feeling his horse gives him from the exercise.

3. Both the horse and rider learn through repeating and perfecting the execution of the pattern.

How many times should one ride and train a pattern? What is recommended? It depends on the rider's and the horse's level of training and their ability to receive instruction. The training should never be boring! The horse's tendency to anticipate is a good sign, meaning that he has begun to understand and that it is time to change to an other exercise pattern.

EXERCISES FOR TRAINING LEVEL

TRAINING LEVEL:
The Foundation

*The figures are the oval, the counter,
leg-yielding in walk, and 20 meter circles. The
cones are set up (small traffic cones
of different colors, usually orange)
in the arena.*

*One of my students once said to me, "A
dressage arena without the cones is like an
apartment without furniture."*

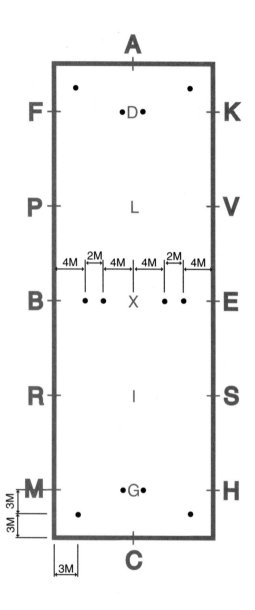

TRAINING LEVEL PATTERN 1
The Oval

TO WARM UP, RISING TROT,
BOTH DIRECTIONS

PURPOSE
A sample for warm up

*"Ride your horse forward
and make him straight!"*

Imagine
Entering the long side
= **entering** a freeway.

Entering the half circle
= **exiting** the freeway.

On the long side: Uphill,
forward, straight.

On the half circle: Round,
longer and lower.

Variation
Ride a single serpentine loop
through the gate of cones in
front of **B** or **E**.

Break the line on the long side.

Observe
How the riders begin to understand how to navigate
and direct their horses.

That the horses steadily begin to "find their backs" and
their footfall.

That the horses work in a relaxed manner and find
their rhythm.

That the work is performed on an oval, thus avoiding
deep corners.

TRAINING LEVEL PATTERN 2
Counter Leg-Yielding

PURPOSE
Basic exercise to introduce the leg-yielding. Ridden on both reins. Also used for introducing and explaining the aids for the half halt.

Explanation
The inside leg at the girth displaces the forehand.

The outside leg, in combination with the outside rein, keeps the horse *forward and straight.*

The whip in the inner hand is used, if necessary, sensitively at the inner hind leg in order to teach the horse to yield the hind leg.

Both reins delicately shuttle the bit to keep the horse relaxed and supple in the neck, the poll (at the axis joint), the jaws and the mouth.

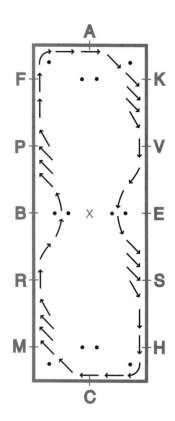

Observe
That the exercise begins in walk.

That the exercise can be executed later in trot, when the horse has learned to perform it correctly in walk.

That the horse must be rewarded as soon as he either understands or improves: *the spontaneous reward!* This means to immediately interrupt the leg-yielding and *either* ride straight ahead along the track *or* make a single serpentine loop and bring the horse back toward the track and continue the training.

TRAINING LEVEL PATTERN 3
The 20 Meter Circle

PURPOSE

To introduce and train the work both at **A**, the center, **X**, and at **C**, circles both in trot and in canter.

Observe

That the rider — thanks to the cones set up — must navigate and, like jumpers and eventers, look for the next fence.

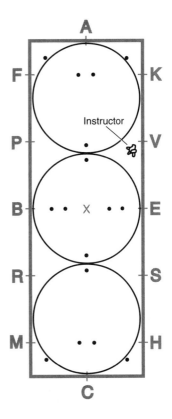

That the rider is instructed to imagine riding the circle in a modified diamond or pentagon shape. This straightening of the horse's body between each "mini-corner," avoids the horse's normal tendency to collapse in the inner base of his neck and to "pop" over the outside shoulder.

That the instructor usually stands outside the circle to observe and control the rider's correct seat and position. The rider must work hard with cen-tripetal (outside) aids to limit the effect of the centrifugal power (which, of course, is amplified at the canter), power which both pushes him to the outside of the horse and pushes the horse off the circumference of the circle.

TRAINING LEVEL · PATTERN 4
The 20 Meter Circle

PURPOSE

To train riding at the 20 meter **L** circle and the 20 meter **I** circle. To train changing circles at **X** and at the same time changing rein as in riding a figure 8.

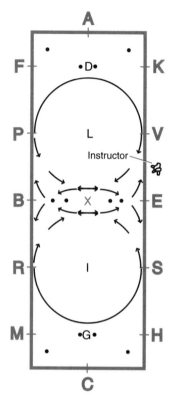

Explanation

The pattern can be ridden both in the trot and the canter.

When switching circles and changing the rein at the canter, it should be performed as change of lead through the trot.

Observe

For the basic observations, review the **Observations** under **Pattern 3**.

That, when switching from one circle, one rides straight for a couple of steps when approaching the center line.

That the rider should emphasize the horse's obedience to the pushing effect of the new outside aids. The horse must learn to follow the rider's weight aids to change direction. Only *then* should the positioning at the poll and the bend be changed.

That the rider does not allow the horse to collapse in the base of his neck and pop over his outside shoulder.

That the rider limits the horse's inclination to lean towards the wall and to follow the track on the long side. The wall *always* has a magnetic influence!

Basic Advice

"Ride your horse forward and make him straight!" This advice is true even when riding circles.

TRAINING LEVEL PATTERN 5
The 20 Meter Circle

PURPOSE
To teach the horse longitudinal stretching and the rider how to let the horse gradually take the rein out of the riders hands.

Explanation
As in **Training Level, Pattern 4**, work in both trot and canter on the **L** and **I** circles. This is more demanding than training the circles at **A** or **C**.

Observe
That the rider navigates correctly *(discipline!)* and is able to control his weight aids to ride his horse forward and make him straight.

Remember, however, horses are strong and smart! For that reason, it is often advisable to instruct riders to imagine riding a circle with the shape of a diamond or a pentagon. This image helps the rider to remember to control the horse's outside and to control the centrifugal forces.

Advice
When performing patterns described above, it is advisable to position the horse at the poll to the outside, like riding an outside shoulder-fore.

The rider's weight should be moved towards the center of the circle.

The rider's inner leg (which, by virtue of the counter-positioning of the horse, is now on the outside of the circle) is placed at the girth and displaces the horse's shoulder and elbow.

The outside rein (the rein closer to the center of the circle) guides the horse along the circumference with an opening effect as necessary. Both reins create obedience when the rider's half halt shifts the center of gravity to the rear and more on to the horse's stifle on the side towards the circle's center.

Observe

That the rider acts positively — with spontaneous rewards — as soon as the horse responds the to aids.

That the rider, when the horse responds to the aids and starts to find his back, his rhythm and his footfall, releases the reins to straighten and allow the horse to gradually stretch forward and down.

That the rider sits at the summit of the horse's topline.

That the horse's profile looks like a rainbow.

That the horse seems to like to eat sand!

Then, *the body-building of the horse has begun!*

EXERCISES FOR FIRST LEVEL

FIRST LEVEL:
The Suppling Work

The figures are leg-yielding,
15 and 10 meter circles, and the lengthening
in the trot.

FIRST LEVEL PATTERN 1
"The Wash Sponge Exercise"

PURPOSE

To train the quarter and half turn on the forehand before training the leg-yielding. This exercise could be used in almost every training situation all the way up to Grand Prix, whenever the horse doesn't pay attention to or respect the rider's inner leg (the hammer).

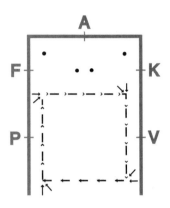

It also trains both the horse and the rider to understand the mechanics of the half halt.

Explanation

To check the horse's attention for the pushing and yielding aids, begin with the turn on the forehand. In every corner of a 15 meter square, the rider performs a quarter turn on the forehand, first to the left, and later to the right. To change the rein, the rider makes a half turn on the forehand in one of the corners. Begin to train the quarter turn from a halt, step by step, and later through the walk.

Observe

That the rider keeps the horse straight in the whole neck except for a slight position at the poll.

That the rider can hardly see more than the horse's eyebrow and nostril.

That the influence on the outside rein keeps the horse from collapsing in the base of his neck.

That the rider uses his yielding inner leg close to the girth.

That the rider carries his whip in his inside hand prepared to use it on the horse's flank.

That the rider keeps the horse moving forward through the whole turn.

That the rider through the turn keeps the horse's jaw and poll supple with a discreet shuttling of the bit.

Thus, the rider has the feeling of wringing tension and resistance out of the horse like wringing a wet was sponge at the sink. Sensitive interactions among the motivating inner leg, the redirecting and modifying outer leg, the receiving and regulating outside hand, and the loosening, suppling inside hand, all in the context of forward thought and connection, can root out many points of resistance through the length of the horse.

FIRST LEVEL PATTERN 2
"The Box Turn"

PURPOSE
To develop the horse's attention to the pushing, yielding
and stopping aids.

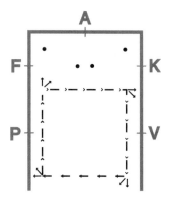

Explanation
In every corner of a 15 meter
square, stop the horse. Ask
him to move only his forehand
in a quarter turn on the
haunches. Ask the horse to
"spin" like a Western-trained
cutting horse. Don't worry if
the horse gets "stuck" in his
hind legs in this exercise.

Observe
That the rider begins to turn the horse using his weight aids
in the direction of the turn, with the outside seat bone
towards the middle of the saddle.

That the rider uses his outside leg close to the girth, in order
to yield the horse's outside shoulder.

That the rider keeps the horse's neck straight except for a
slight position to the turning side at the horse's poll.

That the rider keeps the horse on the spot with both reins.

That the rider shuttles the bit throughout the whole turn to
keep the horse's mouth, jaws and axis joint loose and supple.

That the rider turns the horse step by step and prohibits
anticipation either through a halt or the use of the counter-
bending outside rein. (Comment: counter-bending means
bending to the opposite direction).

The correct performance of this exercise gets the horse to shift
his weight back and prepares him to proceed in trot out of the
turn with good propulsion and self-carriage.

A further exercise based on the box turn is to proceed in the collected trot after the turn and make a downward transition into a halt, and then turn.

FIRST LEVEL PATTERN 3
Preparatory Exercise for Leg-Yielding

PURPOSE
To introduce the leg-yielding in rising trot; also, to introduce a good warm up exercise.

Explanation
Ride the horse in rising trot forward and straight on the diagonal from **M** to **X**. At **X**, continue in rising trot on the diagonal and begin to displace the horse towards the corner at **K**. At **F**, ride the horse forward and straight to **X** in rising trot. At **X**, continue in rising trot on the diagonal and begin to displace the horse towards the corner at **H**.

Observe
That the rider correctly navigates *(discipline!)*.

That the rider keeps his eyes on the focal point, that is, the end of the diagonal.

That the rider puts his weight in the outside stirrup so that the horse follows his weight, but can switch his weight momentarily back to the inside to reinforce the driving leg, if needed.

That the rider keeps his horse straight, except for a slight position at the poll.

That the rider displaces the horse's center of gravity — the forehand — towards the corner.

That the rider uses his inner leg close behind the girth.

That the rider interrupts the displacement if the horse collapses at the inner side or deviates from the line, and rides
instead straight ahead towards the corner rather than trying
to correct the horse during the displacement.

FIRST LEVEL PATTERN 4
Leg-Yielding

PURPOSE
To train the leg-yielding as well as the interruption of the leg-yielding, at first in walk and later in trot.

Explanation
Leg-yielding is a lateral movement along a straight line from start to finish. The rider must follow that line exactly! The horse is ridden through the corner onto the diagonal to keep his forward desire and to get him to understand the direction. The younger the horse, the more important it is for him to understand the *line* and the *focal point* before starting to displace laterally.

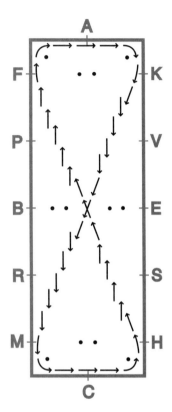

Observe
That the rider *navigates* and keeps his eyes at the focal point in the far end of the diagonal.

That the rider, after a half-halt, applies the outside aids and starts to yield about four steps. I call this a "segment."

That, after the four steps, the rider interrupts the leg-yielding, turns the horse towards the focal point, and follows the line.

That the rider, when the horse is straight and moves forward with a light forehand, begins a new segment of four steps of leg-yielding.

That about three segments of leg-yielding per diagonal is enough.

28

The interruption in the movement teaches the rider to use his outside and pushing aids and to think forward.

The interruption prevents the horse from collapsing in the base of his neck and from popping over the outside shoulder, or from deviating from the line and perhaps losing his desire to move.

Now, the rider begins to "dance" with his horse!

FIRST LEVEL PATTERN 5
Leg-Yielding

PURPOSE
To train leg yielding from "start" to "finish," after a 15 meter half-circle.

Explanation
Start at **H** and follow the track towards **E**. At **E**, begin a 15 meter half-circle towards the cones (gate of cones) on the far side of the center line. At the cone gate, ride the diagonal line back towards **H** and execute the leg-yielding away from the right leg. At **M**, continue the exercise in the opposite direction via **B**.

Observe
That the rider *navigates!*

That the rider makes a careful, round half-circle.

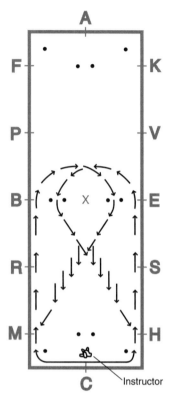

That the rider allows the horse to pass through the gate of cones and helps the horse be aware of the "line" towards the corner.

That the rider applies the outside aids before he starts to leg-yield.

That the leg-yielding is performed with the horse's front legs on the "line," without any deviation whatsoever.

If the horse, in spite of the rider's attempts to avoid it, starts to deviate from the "line," the rider must decisively interrupt the leg-yielding and ride the horse forward and straight towards the corner.

My Recommendation:

Sometimes, allow the rider to use his whip in the outside hand. When or if the horse shows a tendency to lose his desire to move forward or to yield, ask the rider to touch the horse on the outside flank. Usually, that touch gives an immediate and obvious positive reaction!

This exercise is an example of when the rider repeats a pattern.

Advantages

1. The instructor does not need to tell what to do all the time.

2. It is a good example of learning by doing both for the horse and the rider.

3. The instructor is able to concentrate on teaching how to and why!!

How many times ? What is recommended?

It depends on the rider's and the horse's level of training and ability to receive instruction.

It should never be boring! Remember, the horse's tendency to anticipate is a good sign that he has begun to understand and that it is time to change to an other exercise.

FIRST LEVEL PATTERN 6
Leg-Yielding in Combination with the Canter Depart

PURPOSE

To train the leg-yielding from the beginning in the corner to the finish at the gate of cones, combining it with a strike-off in the canter.

Explanation

Begin at **M** on the diagonal towards the two cones (the gate of cones) on the far side of the centerline. On the diagonal, execute the leg-yielding. At the cone gate, strike off in a left lead canter on a 15 meter half-circle towards **B**. At **R**, make a transition to working trot. At **H**, begin leg-yielding towards the other cone gate. In the cone gate, strike off in the right lead canter on a 15 meter half-circle towards **E**. At **S**, make the transition to working trot.

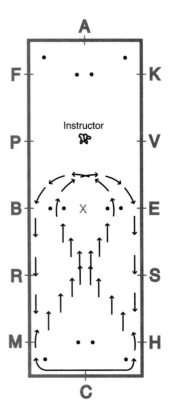

Observe

That the rider *navigates!*

That the rider picks up the diagonal and shows the horse the cone gate before he starts to leg-yield.

That the rider applies the outside aids before he starts the leg-yielding.

That the leg-yielding is performed on the line without any deviation whatsoever.

This is competitive training!

That at the canter strike off, the rider looks — glances — over his outside shoulder to avoid collapsing his inside waistline and moves his outside seat bone to the middle of the saddle.

That the aids for the canter strike-off are given just when the horse is inside the cone gate and beginning to turn towards the wall.

First Level Patterns 1 through **6** are good suppling exercises for upper level horses and could be used often. Performed correctly, they encourage horses to more *forward* as well as laterally, promoting straightness, lightness of the forehand, and obedience to the legs.

This is a good foundation for the lateral movements in collected trot.

FIRST LEVEL PATTERN 7
10 and 15 Meter Circles

PURPOSE
To train 10 and 15 meter circles.

Explanation

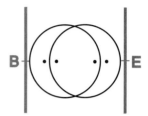

Train 15 meter circles either from **E** or **B** through the cone gate on the far quarter line or from the cone gate at the quarter line towards **E** or **B**.

Train 10 meter circles from **X** towards **E** or **B**.

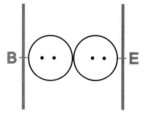

Train 10 meter circles either from **E** or **B**.

Train 10 meter circles from quarter line to quarter line.

Observe

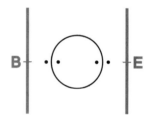

That the rider *navigates* and from his high position "draws" the circles with his eyes. The horse then follows the rider's eyes!

That the rider makes the second half of the circle as equally large and round as the first half.

That the rider uses his weight aids (the outside seat bone in the middle of the saddle) to encourage the horse to enter the circle.

That the rider *allows* the horse to follow the weight aids when releasing the outside rein.

That the rider guides the horse along the circle with the inner rein.

That the rider never allows the horse to collapse in the base of the neck, or to pop over the outside shoulder.

Remember
Even when riding circles,

Ride your horse forward and make him straight!

FIRST LEVEL PATTERN 8
20 Meter Circles with Canter Strike-Off

PURPOSE

To train the riding of a 20 meter circle at the trot, changing the rein inside the 20 meter circle via **X**, and then at **X**, striking off in the canter when changing rein.

Explanation

Ride the 20 meter circle on the left rein. Begin to change rein at **E**, following a 10 meter half-circle left.

Come up straight on the center line facing **C**, and strike off in the right lead canter, following a 10 meter half-circle towards **B**. Follow the 20 meter circle on the right lead for about two laps.

After a downward transition to trot, repeat the pattern starting either at **E** or at **B**.

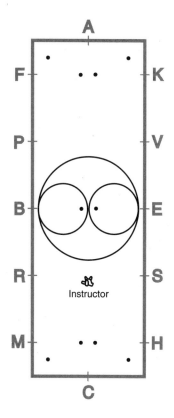

Observe

That the rider allows the horse to enter the 10 meter half-circle at **E**.

That the rider at **X** switches his weight from left to right and looks (glances) over his outside shoulder, when he strikes off in the canter.

That the rider doesn't prohibit—block—the canter strike-off with the new inside (old outside) rein.

That the rider *allows* the horse to strike off when he releases the new outside rein.

35

FIRST LEVEL PATTERN 9
Lengthening Strides in Trot

PURPOSE
To train the lengthening as well as the shortening of the strides in trot. Also, to train transitions.

Explanation
The drawing describes training on the left rein.

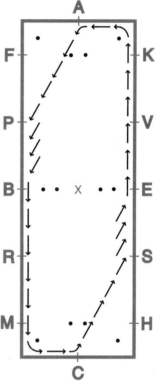

Ride a deep corner at **K**. Keep the inside flexion and suppleness from the corner to the center line. At **A**, begin to cut a second corner towards **P**, and to make the horse straight using the outside rein.

At the same time, begin to push the horse forward with the outside right leg at the girth. When the horse reacts forward, complete the pushing aids with the inner leg at the girth.

Most horses easily understand that they are being asked to lengthen their stride when they are pushed forward from the bent and flexed position.

Approaching the wall at **P**, avoid pulling the reins for a downward transition. Remember, the wall is an "anvil."

Prepare and then finish in a counter leg-yielding. See again **Training Level, Pattern 2, *Counter Leg-Yielding.***

Observe
That the rider *navigates!*

That the rider gets the horse to react forward with good energy. Some horses are lazy and proceed only with a third or half of their ability. In that situation, the rider must decisively push the horse in to an energetic and fairly fast canter to regain discipline. After a couple "wake up calls," the horse normally starts to work well.

That the rider is "brave" enough to keep the horse straight at the wall and let the wall teach the horse the collection and downward transition.

That the rider learns to feel the horse's response for the collection and tries to make the counter leg-yielding situation as brief as possible.

Don't forget: *spontaneous rewards!*

My Advice
When training lengthening of strides in trot think, "Short distance. Good quality." Save the long diagonals for the tests at shows.

Comment
A horse never covers more ground—takes longer steps—than he is able to reach with his nose!

Riding a horse deep or over-flexed at times promotes the use of his back. But witness horses at the trotting track who are driven with an over-check to keep their heads up and their noses in front of the vertical to enhance the shoulder freedom and the length of the stride. In training, it is our duty to combine these two ideas.

FIRST LEVEL PATTERN 10
Lengthening Strides in Trot

PURPOSE
To train the lengthening of strides in trot out of the leg-yielding or shoulder-in along the wall.

Explanation
Start at **A** on the right rein. From **K** to **V**, ride the leg-yielding with the right leg or a shoulder-in right.

At **V** towards **R** on the diagonal, ride the lengthening of strides.

At **R**, ride a transition to working trot through the counter leg-yielding until the horse understands and obeys the downward transition and collection. Review **Training Level, Pattern 2** and **First Level, Pattern 9**.

At **H** to **S**, ride a leg-yielding with the left leg or a shoulder-in left. At **S** on the diagonal towards **P**, ride the lengthening of strides.

At **P**, make the transition to working trot through counter leg-yielding until the horse understands and obeys the downward transition and collection.

Observe
That the rider *navigates!*

That the rider gets the horse to react forward with energy. Again, some horses are lazy and will only offer a third or a half of their ability. In that situation, the rider must decisively push the horse into an energetic and fairly fast canter to get discipline. After a couple of "wake up calls," the work normally begins to improve.

That the rider is "brave" enough to keep the horse straight at the wall and let the wall teach the horse the collection and the downward transition.

That the rider learns to feel the horse's response for the collection and tries to make the counter leg-yielding situation as short as possible.

Don't forget: *spontaneous rewards!*

My Advice

When training lengthening of strides in trot think "Short distance. Good quality." Save the long diagonals for the tests at shows.

FIRST LEVEL PATTERN 11
Leg-Yielding and Lengthening in Trot

PURPOSE
To combine the suppling exercise of leg-yielding with the lengthening of the strides in trot.

Explanation
Begin at **A** in the trot on the right rein. At **K**, ride onto the diagonal and proceed in a leg-yielding from the left leg.

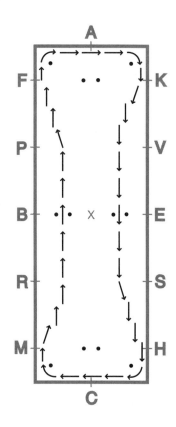

Reaching the quarter line, use the outside rein to make the horse straight. At the same time apply the outside leg at the girth and push the horse forward. Ride straight ahead through the cone gate.

Begin a downward transition. To avoid any kind of resistance, begin leg-yielding towards the long side and the corner at **H**. At **M**, move onto the diagonal and proceed in a leg-yielding from the left leg.

Repeat the pattern on the opposite side.

Observe
That the rider allows the horse to move onto the diagonal before he starts the leg-yielding along the diagonal.

That the rider — when interrupting the leg-yielding and beginning to lengthen the strides— asks for a good and steady contact on the outside rein, where he *learns to feel* if the horse has the desire to move forward or not.

That if the horse is repeatedly lazy, the rider should push him quickly into an energetic canter a couple of times.

Also review **First Level, Patterns 9** and **10**.

Photo courtesy of United States Dressage Federation, Inc.

EXERCISES FOR SECOND LEVEL

SECOND LEVEL:
Introducing Collection

*The figures are the rein back,
the shoulder-in, the travers, the counter-canter,
and the half-turn on the haunches.*

SECOND LEVEL PATTERN 1
The Rein Back

PURPOSE
Rein back in most other languages is explained or translated as "the backwards walk." "Backwards walk" correctly suggests to the rider that the horse must accept the forward pushing aids to be able to walk backwards on the bit.

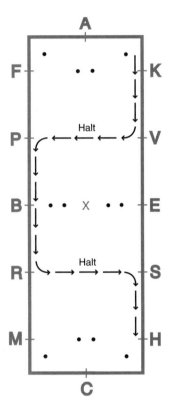

Explanation
Begin at the walk and turn anywhere on the long side onto the center line. Prepare and make a halt at the center line. After the halt, train the rein back 3 - 4 steps. Later, work from the trot and canter.

Change rein frequently.

Observe
That at the halt the horse is well on the aids, standing square.

That the rider gives forward pushing aids, with both legs close to the girth.

That when the horse moves his center of gravity forward, the rider meets the horse's forward reaction with a non-allowing hand, shuttling the bit.

That the rider, when the horse translates the aids and begins to walk backwards, gives spontaneous rewards with softening fingers at each step.

Comments
If the horse is not well on the aids and squared at the front feet, *don't even try the rein back!*

If after the halt the horse doesn't accept the pushing aids forward, *don't even try the rein back!* Instead, proceed forward and get the horse in front of the legs.

Try to avoid nervously leaning forward, moving the legs backwards to the flanks, and starting to pull.

If the horse is tense and resistant, try one of these two approaches. The first is to begin a quarter turn on the forehand. When the horse lifts the hind leg, squeeze the same side rein. The horse usually makes one step backwards. Continue like that — alternating left and right side carefully — and be pleased with a little progress.

Or, use a ground person, who cooperates with the rider as explained above and who gives the horse sugar or carrot at every successful attempt. Sometimes the ground person can carefully tap the horse on the pastern or the cannon bone with a short riding whip.

Always try to create confidence! Avoid all violence. Avoid, in the beginning, working on the track or along the wall.

If horse does not walk backwards straight, do not correct him with the lower legs. Such an attempt normally creates only resistance.

Instead, try to get the forehand in front of the rear end using guiding reins. Imagine going backwards with a car or a truck.

SECOND LEVEL PATTERN 2
Shoulder-In

PURPOSE

A preparatory exercise to
explain to the rider how to
achieve the correct bending for
the shoulder-in. Also, a stretching, aerobic gymnastic. To help
the rider develop the ability to
ride concentric 5 meter circle(s)
in the walk.

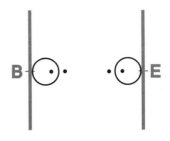

Explanation

To ride a concentric 5 meter
circle in walk around a cone
seems to be a simple task. In my experience, even riders with
good routine have problems keeping the circle *concentric* and
in managing their weight aids correctly through the whole
circle.

Every time the horse lifts his inner hind leg, he elevates his
inner croup. This gives the rider a push, moving him to the
outside of the horse's back. It means the rider must correct
his weight aids almost every step. Think "Bun Management!"
It is a good way to repeat the basic elements for how to correctly turn a horse: follow my weight, follow my leading rein,
and respect my inner leg.

The goal is to stretch the horse's outside, thus achieving the
bending of the inside. The horse should follow— without any
resistance—the rider's weight and the leading rein, which
allows for the contraction of the rib cage and flank around
the inner leg. Train the exercise on both hands.

Observe

That the rider keeps the horse on the same circle all the time.

That the rider keeps his inner weight — the outside seat bone
in the middle of the saddle — correctly on the inside for the
whole circle. Think *"Bun Management!"*

That the inner leg at the girth (the hammer) creates contraction of the horse's rib cage and flank.

That the passive outside leg is applied behind the girth (the anvil).

That the inner rein leads the horse to follow the circumference of the circle.

Frequently, the rider must ask the horse to "look at his tail," moving the inside hand with a leading, opening gesture downward, away from the neck, and behind the rider's thigh. As the horse is learning to stretch his outside muscles, overbending of the neck to the inside is desirable, but even though the outside shoulder is more open (or bulging) than normal, the horse must not be allowed to escape from the chosen line.

That the outside rein allows (no contact!) the horse to follow the inner rein.

That the rider does not try to correct the horse's attempts to pop over his outside shoulder with the outside rein. It is a frequently occurring, but wrong reaction when the horse refuses to follow the inner rein.

Check
That when the rider extends the inner rein and gives a *spontaneous reward,* the horse keeps stretching in the neck and outside rib cage, while staying on the actual circle. The horse is supposed to be depending on and obeying the rider's seat, weight and legs — not the rein!

SECOND LEVEL PATTERN 3
Shoulder-In

PURPOSE
A preparatory exercise to explain to the rider how to achieve the correct bending for the shoulder-in. Also, to teach the rider to change direction using his weight and leg aids, supported by a leading, guiding and generously rewarding inner rein.

Explanation
This stretching and aerobic gymnastic develops the rider's ability to ride concentric 5 meter figure eight circles. It is a kind of basic exercise in order to train the rider to be able to quickly change his weight aids from one side of the horse's back to the other. The weight aids are the most essential and most influential, but also the most subtle and least noticeable. The more advanced dressage training, the more critical the correct use of the weight aids.

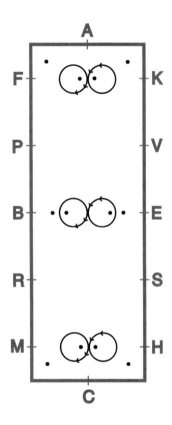

Observe
That the rider keeps his weight — the outside seat bone in the middle of the saddle — on the inside correctly for the entire circle. *"Bun Management!"*

That the inner leg at the girth (the hammer) creates contraction of the horse's rib cage and flank.

That the passive outside leg is applied behind the girth (the anvil).

That the inner rein leads the horse to follow the circumference of the circle.

Frequently, the rider must ask the horse to "look at his tail," moving his hand with the leading rein downwards and outside his thigh.

That the out side rein allows (no contact) the horse to follow the inner rein.

Check

That when the rider extends the inner rein and gives a *spontaneous reward,* the horse keeps stretching in the neck and outside rib cage, while staying on the actual circle. The horse is supposed to be depending on and obeying the rider's seat, weight and legs — not the rein!

SECOND LEVEL PATTERN 4
Shoulder-In

PURPOSE
To begin and then interrupt
the shoulder-in, first at the
walk, later at the trot. To teach
the rider the correct use of, and
to develop the horse's attention
and obedience to, the aids for
the half halt as well as for the
halt. Train on both hands.

Explanation
Ride a 5 meter circle in the
corner. Compare with **Second
Level, Patterns 2** and **3**.

After the circle in the corner,
come as if entering the diagonal at **K**, creating an angle of
about 35 degrees. Make a halt
with the horse on the aids and
with the correct bend for the
shoulder-in right.

After the halt, proceed in
shoulder-in right, ride another
circle and make another halt in
the shoulder-in right position.

After the halt, proceed in shoulder-in right, ride another
circle. After the circle, begin a 20 meter half-circle from
E to **B**. Via **P, F** and **A**, return to the corner at **K** and repeat
the exercise.

Observe
That the rider *navigates!*

That the rider should create an equal bending through the
horse.

That the rider doesn't allow the horse to collapse in the base of the neck or to pop over his outside shoulder.

Recommendations

Train the halt checking that the rider has the horse on the aids and especially noting the influence of the outside leg (the anvil).

Don't try to squeeze in everything in the first training session.

Train the pattern until the rider and the horse begin to understand and improve. The horse's anticipation is a good sign. For that reason, *don't punish anticipation!*

SECOND LEVEL PATTERN 5
Shoulder-In

PURPOSE
To train the shoulder-in along the wall on the right hand. Remember, *Short distance — Good quality!*

Observe
The suggestion for the instructor's position in the arena.

That the circle in the corner is correctly performed.

That, at first, the rider creates an angle of about 45 degrees, which is later gently decreased to the preferred angle of about 30 degrees.

The reason for this is that it is easy to decrease the angle, but sometimes impossible to increase the angle when training along the track. Horses like to lean their outside rib cage and hind leg towards the wall for support for their balance.
The wall or fence exert magnetic influence upon the horse!

That the rider should ride on the second track (about four feet off the wall) to prohibit the horse from leaning into the wall. This requires the rider to use his outside leg (the anvil).

That the horse steps forward with his inner hind leg and passes it in front of the outside hind in order to be able to carry his center of gravity at the shoulder and withers.

That the rider looks ahead, navigates and prepares either to ride forward in working trot along the 20 meter half-circle **V** to **P**, or to strike off in the right lead canter at **V** on the 10 meter half-circle towards the center line at **L**, prepared to repeat the pattern in trot at **A**.

That the pattern should be trained on the left hand as well, beginning in the corner at **F**.

SECOND LEVEL PATTERN 6
Shoulder-In and Transitions to Medium Trot

PURPOSE
To train the shoulder-in and to control the horse's desire to move straight and forward out of the shoulder-in.

Observe
That the rider *navigates*.

That the shoulder-in is performed on the second track (about four feet off the track).

Suggestion
Note the instructor's position.

Review **First Level, Patterns 7** and **8**.

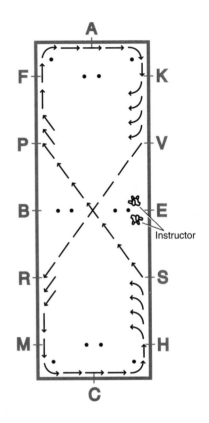

Instructor

SECOND LEVEL PATTERN 7
Shoulder-In at the Center Line

PURPOSE

To train the shoulder-in at
the center line — preferably
towards and in front of a
mirror — emphasizing the use
of the outside leg. The rider's
outside leg maintains the
direction of the hind legs
along the center line.

Explanation

Begin at **H** on the left rein
in collected trot. At **E**, ride a
10 meter half-circle left and
prepare for shoulder-in left
down the center line from **X** to
G. At **G**, turn left and repeat the
pattern about three times. After
the third time, turn right at G
and train the shoulder-in right
down the center line.

Observe

That the rider *navigates.*

That the rider establishes the
bending, establishes the angle,
and performs a successful half
halt before he proceeds along the center line.

That the lightness of the forehand should be obvious.

That the poll is supposed to be the highest point of the neck.

That the horse's hind legs follow the center line.

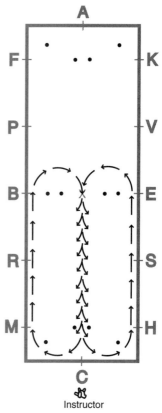

Instructor

SECOND LEVEL PATTERN 8
Travers (Haunches-In)

"THE SNOW PLOW"

PURPOSE
To train the travers left along
the wall after a 6 meter circle
in the corner and a relaxing 10
meter circle at half the distance.

Explanation
Start in collected walk at **K**
on the left rein. In the corner
just before **F**, ride a 6 meter
circle. At **F**, proceed in travers
left. At **P**, ride a 10 meter circle
to refresh the gait. After the
circle, continue the travers left.
At **B**, release the horse into a
working trot on a 20 meter half-
circle from **B** to **E**. Repeat the
pattern at **K**.

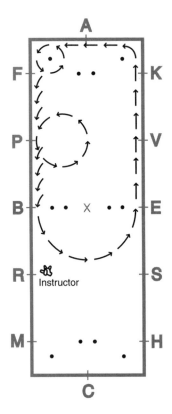

After establishing the pattern at
the walk, train the pattern in
the trot.

Later, train the pattern on the
other hand, beginning in the
corner by **F** and riding travers right from **K**, first in the walk
and then in the trot.

Observe
That the corner circle is correct (evenly round), and creates
flexibility in the bending.

That the rider and the horse have the same focal point in the
far corner at **M**.

That the rider keeps the horse's outside jaw parallel with the
wall.

That the rider waits to bring the haunches in (the construction of a snow plow) until the horse looks down the track.

That when performing the travers, the rider keeps the horse looking down the track all the time. Horses will *always* try to look either in towards the arena, or out towards the wall in order to try to avoid holding the bend for the travers.

Suggestion
Note the recommendation of an appropriate position for the instructor.

Advice
When performing the travers, the rider should think of using the aids for shoulder-in — which means using the inner leg at the girth as the hammer!

SECOND LEVEL PATTERN 9
Travers (Haunches-In)
"The Snow Plow"

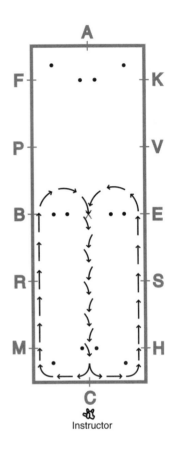

PURPOSE
A preparatory Exercise for the half pass. To train the travers at the center line, preferably, in front of a mirror, and to both the left and the right.

Explanation
Begin on the left rein at **H** in collected trot. At **E**, make a 10 meter half-circle left and prepare to ride travers left down the center line. Between **X** and **G**, ride travers left.

At **G**, turn left and repeat the pattern about three times. The third time, turn right at **G** and train travers right down the center line **X** to **G**.

Observe
That, coming down the center line, both the rider and the horse look directly at **C**. The rider keeps looking in to the instructor's eyes.

That the horse's front legs absolutely follow the center line.

That the horse works on three or four tracks and is not allowed to exaggerate the yielding of the hind legs.

Suggestion
Note the indication of an appropriate position for the instructor.

Advice
The rider, when riding the travers, should think of using the aids for shoulder-in—which means to use the inner leg at the girth as a *hammer*.

SECOND LEVEL PATTERN 10
The Travers and the Half Pass

PURPOSE

To help the rider understand that the half pass is simply travers performed along a diagonal line, and that the aids are the same as those used for the travers. To be worked in both directions.

Explanation

Begin at M on the right rein in collected trot. At A, turn down the center line and ride travers to the right from **D** to **X**. At **X**, begin to ride half pass right towards **M**.

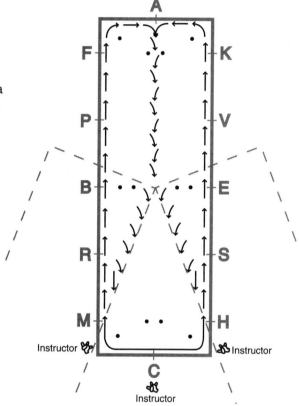

Finish the half pass with a few steps of leg-yielding from the left leg to get the horse straight and forward. At **H**, repeat the pattern on the left rein.

Observe

That the rider *navigates!*

That the horse looks exactly at the finish of every line!

That, at **X**, the rider carefully rides the horse through a soft turn on one track before he applies the aids for the half pass on the new line of **X** to **H** or **X** to **M** so to prevent the hind legs

---

from leading in the new direction — a severe fault!

That the horse's front legs absolutely follow the track. No deviation whatsoever is to be accepted.

That the rider interrupts every half pass with some encouraging steps of leg-yielding to regain the forward movement and to increase impulsion in the trot.

Suggestion
Note the indication of an appropriate position for the instructor during each phase of the exercise.

My Advice
All lateral movements should follow a straight line between the start and finish. Try to establish "competitive" training right from the very beginning!

SECOND LEVEL PATTERN 11
"The Bow Tie"

PURPOSE

To combine the work at half
and full circles (10 or 15 meters)
with the schooling of shoulder-
in, travers and half pass.

Explanation

Begin out of a circle at **E** to
the left towards **K**. From **E** to **K**,
ride travers. At **K**, begin the 10
meter half-circle left back
towards **D**. From **D** to **E**, ride
half pass left.

At **E**, ride either a 10 or a 15
meter circle right. At **E**, ride
shoulder-in right. At **H**, begin
a 10 meter half-circle right
towards **G**. From **G** to **E**, ride
half pass or the leg-yielding.

Then at **E**, ride a 10 or 15 meter
circle left and start the pattern
again at **E**.

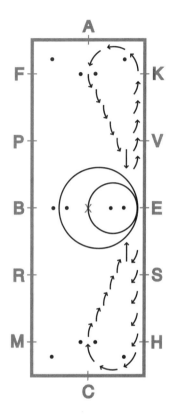

My Advice

Avoid beginning the half pass
before the horse has completed the 10 meter half-circle and is
approaching **E**. If the rider gives the aids for the half pass too
early, the horse anticipates and often the hind legs lead the
movement. A severe fault! Finish the half pass with some
steps in leg-yielding to keep the horse straight and forward,
before he enter the circle at **E**.

Comment

This pattern can be successfully used for all kinds of students
and horses. The dressage movements inside the pattern must of
course be adapted to the riders and the horses level of training.

SECOND LEVEL PATTERN 12
Counter-Canter

PURPOSE
To school the strike off in the counter-canter and to make downward transitions to trot.

Explanation
Proceed in working trot on the left hand at **M**. At **C**, pass through the corner at **H** around the corner cone (No.1). Perform a shallow serpentine loop around the second cone (No. 2).

Strike off in the right lead counter-canter. At **V**, begin the downward transition to trot. At **K**, proceed in trot and repeat the exercise on the next long side from **F** to **R**.

Observe
That the rider navigates and avoids looking down to the inner side in the counter-canter strike off to avoid collapsing in his waist line.

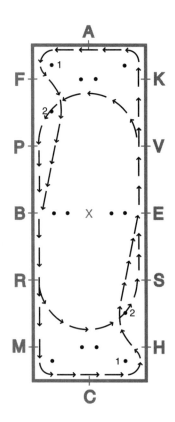

That the rider gives the aids for the counter-canter strike off when he begins the shallow serpentine loop around the second cone; i.e., when the bend changes and the horse's weight shifts direction.

That the rider, when he begins the downward transition to trot, flexes the horse towards the wall and regulates the horse's movement towards the wall with his outside leg. He places the horse as if in a narrow trap. After some attempts the horse usually starts to obey and to make soft transitions to trot.

Later

School the exercise on the right rein, picking up the left lead counter-canter. Move the No. 2 cones to the opposite side of the school (what will now be the No. 1 cones are already in place).

SECOND LEVEL PATTERN 13
Counter-Canter

PURPOSE

To combine **Pattern 12** with a 20 meter half-circle in counter-canter.

Explanation

Train **Pattern 12** until the down transitions to trot are consistently satisfactory. Then add a 20 meter half-circle in counter canter either from **V** or **R**.

After every successful half-circle in counter-canter, make a transition to trot at **B** or **E** with spontaneous rewards.

Observe

That the rider *navigates*.

That the rider keeps the horse's neck straight, except for a slight inside position (in the direction of the leading leg) at the poll so the rider is just able to see the horse's eyebrow and nostril.

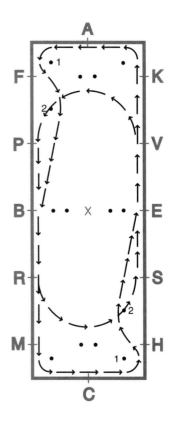

That the rider reinforces the aids for the appropriate lead when riding the 20 meter half-circle in counter-canter.

That the rider applies his outside leg with clear contact, his leg working with a somewhat yielding effect as in travers.

That the rider's outside leg works like a tugboat pushing a big tanker into a new direction.

Later, move the No. 2 cones to the opposite side of the arena to train the left lead counter-canter.

SECOND LEVEL PATTERN 14
Counter-Canter

PURPOSE
To school one half of a 20 meter circle in counter-canter, followed by a refreshing 15 meter circle in the true lead. The sample describes training of the right lead counter-canter.

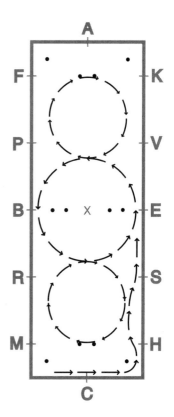

Explanation
Pick up the right lead counter-canter after the corner at **H**. At **E**, enter the center 20 meter circle.

At the center line, switch onto a 15 meter circle to the right in the true lead.

Returning to the center line, proceed in counter-canter on one half of the center 20 meter circle, and at the center line move onto another 15 meter circle in the true lead.

Observe
That the rider *navigates*.

That the rider, beginning the counter-canter, reinforces the aids for the actual lead with the outside leg applied close to the horse's rib cage.

That the rider keeps the horse straight in the neck, except for a slight inside position at the poll.

Later, train the left lead counter-canter, beginning at the corner by **M**.

SECOND LEVEL PATTERN 15
Counter-Canter

PURPOSE
To train the conventional serpentine loops, with no change of lead.

Recommendation
If the horse gets "high" or disobedient, go back and reschool the **Patterns 12, 13** and **14**!

Observe
That the rider *navigates.*

That the horse is ridden up in front of the actual gate of cones fairly soon in the schooling. Then the horse more clearly understands and accepts the aids for the counter-canter.

That the rebalancing aids for the half halts are given *before* the rider intends to turn in to the counter-canter.

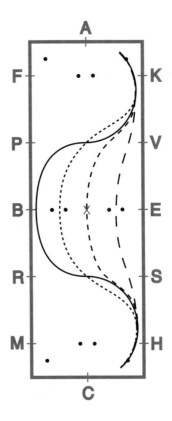

SECOND LEVEL PATTERN 16
The Half Turn on the Haunches

PREPARATORY EXERCISE #1:
THE QUARTER TURN IN WALK
AND THE HALT

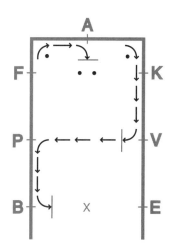

PURPOSE
To begin to introduce the half
turn on the haunches, piece
by piece.

Recommendation
Repeat **First Level, Pattern 1,**
***The Quarter and Half Turn on
the Forehand,*** and **First Level,
Pattern 2,** ***The Box Turn.***

Explanation
The rider performs a soft
quarter turn followed by the
immediate halt before the
cones gate, keeping the horse's inside flexing at the poll and
his suppleness. The drawing demonstrates the first quarter
turn to the right at **A** and illustrates other examples at **V** and
B. After the first quarter turn, the horse is turned back to the
track and is ridden through the corner at **K** for a new quarter
turn to the right at **V**. After the turn, ride straight ahead
toward P for another quarter turn to the left at **B**

Experience
When asking a student to ride a quarter turn followed by
an immediate halt, the student's initial reaction is often
incorrect, owing to nervousness. Incorrectly, he uses the outside rein (neck reining) and his outside leg yields the horse
in to the turn.

However, the half turn on the haunches must start with a
relaxed horse, who is *allowed* to turn (review **First Level,
Pattern 7**), as when he turns down the center line, or makes
a turn from one side of the school to the other.

Recommendation

If the rider doesn't understand the feel of a relaxed quarter turn, let him make a small, 5 meter circle before the quarter turn to feel the horse's contraction in the rib cage and respect for the inner leg. The immediate halt in connection with the quarter turn is intended to help the rider understand the importance of the half halts through the half turn on the haunches later.

Observe

That the rider performs a soft quarter turn, shuttling the bit and keeps the horse's axis joint, jaws and mouth loose and supple.

That the horse pays immediate attention to the aids for the halt.

That at the halt, the rider controls his weight aids, which in the turn are often moved to the wrong side of the horse's back.

SECOND LEVEL PATTERN 17
The Half Turn on the Haunches

PREPARATORY EXERCISE #2

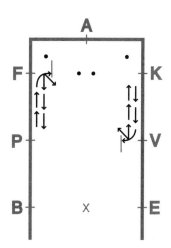

PURPOSE
To train the half turn on the haunches step by step.

Recommendation
Repeat **First Level, Patterns 1** and **2**, as well as **First Level, Pattern 7** and **Second Level, Pattern 16**.

Explanation
The rider performs a soft quarter turn followed by the immediate halt keeping the horse's inside flexion at the poll and his suppleness. After the halt the rider performs the box turn and continues in walk in the new direction.

Observe
That the rider, shuttling the bit, keeps the horse's axis joint, jaws and mouth loose and supple through the quarter turn. If the rider is not yet able to ride a soft quarter turn, have him make a 5 meter circle to prepare the turn.

That the horse obeys the aids for the halt. In some stubborn cases, it might be advisable to rein back a couple of steps to establish discipline and to shift the horse's weight backwards.

That, after the halt, the rider controls the position of his weight aids. If wrong, he corrects by moving his outside seat bone into the middle of the saddle.

That, in the box turn, the rider yields the horse's shoulders with his outside leg close to the girth in order to keep the horse's hind legs more or less on the spot.

Observation

In some cases, if the horse anticipates and falls onto his inner shoulder and through the rider's inside leg, trying to continue the turn on the haunches on his own, he must be stopped, made to stand and may, without reversing the position of the rider's legs or the bend of the horse, be yielded back towards the original line in a *counter turn on the haunches.* This re-establishes discipline for the inner leg.

Comment

When the rider uses his outside leg close to the girth, the leg works as a forward pushing aid. Remember, "Legs *forward* means *forward*," while "Legs *backwards* means *collection*."

When the rider uses his outside leg close to girth, he then also has the initiative and avoids the horse's tendency to be stuck, to yield or step backwards with the inner hind leg.

SECOND LEVEL PATTERN 18
Half Turn on the Haunches

PURPOSE
To school and train the half turn on the haunches, as prepared by **Second Level, Patterns 16** and **17**.

Explanation
Begin to train the pattern as shown at **P** and **V** on the long side. Then continue to school the pattern inside the arena, for instance, between **M** and **H** as asked for in many tests.

Continue the schooling on a 20 meter circle to change the rein, occasionally combined with a strike-off in the true lead canter or the counter-canter.

Observe
That the introduction to the half turn on the haunches is a softly ridden quarter turn. The aids *allow* the horse to turn.

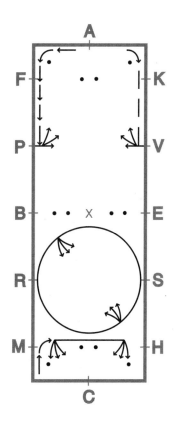

That after the quarter turn, the rider executes the half halts.

That, during the half halts, the rider controls his weight aids, moving his outside seat bone to the middle of the saddle.

That, after the half halts, the rider opens his inner wrist, thus suggesting to the horse the rest of the turn when combined with the outside leg.

That the rider thinks *forward.*

That the rider avoids looking down at the inner side because this normally makes him collapse at the waistline and unable to keep his weight inside through the whole turn.

EXERCISES FOR THIRD LEVEL

THIRD LEVEL:
Increased Collection

*The movements in this level are the
flying change and the half pass.*

THIRD LEVEL PATTERN 1
The Half Pass

AS FOUND IN AHSA
THIRD LEVEL TESTS 1 AND 2

PURPOSE
To train the half pass for
competition, starting from a
half-circle.

Explanation
From **P** to **L**, ride a 10 meter
half-circle right. From **L** to **M**,
ride half pass right. **M** to **H** to
V, follow the track.

From **V** to **L**, ride a 10 meter
half-circle left. From **L** to **H**,
ride half pass left.

Note: The line of dashes in the
illustration describe Third
Level, Test 2.

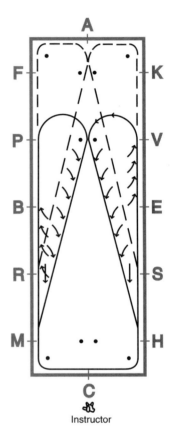

Advice
1. Put two cones as a gate,
   four meters apart, around L
   to indicate the start of the
   half pass.

2. Allow the rider to ride a short distance of travers on the
   long side before he enters the half-circle at **V** or **P** (or at **F**
   or **K**) in order to get the feeling of the "snowplow."

Observe
That the rider begins to navigate at **V** or **P** for the line **L** to **M**,
or **L** to **H**.

That the rider and the horse have the same focal point — the
finish of the line — when beginning the half pass.

That the rider finishes the half-circle and allows the horse onto the diagonal line straight and with good impulsion, before he applies the aids for the half pass, thus avoiding having the haunches lead the lateral movement—a severe fault.

That the rider keeps the horse's front feet on the diagonal line. No deviation whatsoever should be tolerated.

That if the quality of the half-pass decreases, the rider either changes to riding a decisive leg-yielding to improve the horse's desire to move forward and to yield with lightness and elegance, or give the aids for shoulder-in for a couple of steps. Riding half pass right, the rider is prepared to use the aids for shoulder-in right, so this is a good reminder for the horse!

That the rider, when approaching the end of the line (the finish), always interrupts a half pass with some straightening and encouraging steps in leg-yielding in the working trot.

Comment
When performing the travers or the half pass, the horse's blaze or star should shine upon the track the rider has decided to ride like a miner's head lamp!

THIRD LEVEL PATTERN 2
Half Pass in the Trot

AS IN AHSA THIRD LEVEL TEST 3

PURPOSE
To train the half pass, starting diagonally from the track on the long side, as asked for in the test.

Explanation
Begin along the track from either **K** on the right rein, or **F** on the left rein, to ride half pass left from **P** to **I** or half pass right from **V** to **I**.

Advice
Put two cones four meters apart around **I**.

Observe
That the rider—early!—already through the corner at **K** or **F** begins to navigate the lines **V** to **I** or **P** to **I**.

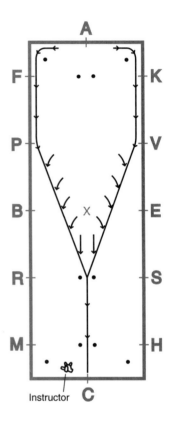

That the rider allows the horse onto the diagonal line with good impulsion *before* he gives the aids for the half pass, thus avoiding the haunches lead the movement—a severe fault.

That the rider makes certain that the horse doesn't collapse in the base of his neck.

That the rider uses his inner leg actively as a hammer, close to the girth, to keep the horse following the line and to keep his inner rib cage contracted.

That the rider keeps the horse on "the line." No deviation should be allowed.

That if the quality of the half pass decreases, the rider either rides a decisive leg-yielding to improve the horse's desire to move forward with lightness and elegance or gives the aids for shoulder-in for a couple of steps. Riding half pass right the rider is prepared to use the aids for shoulder-in right—a good reminder for the horse!

That the rider, when approaching the center line, the finish, always interrupts the half pass with some straightening and encouraging steps of leg-yielding in the working trot.

THIRD LEVEL
The Flying Change of Lead

PREPARATORY EXERCISES

1. Miles of counter-canter.

2. Many simple changes of lead.

3. Frequent training of Second Level, Pattern 12 (the counter-canter on the long sides with the transition to trot before the corner) and Second Level, Pattern 14 (the counter-canter on 20 meter half-circle at the center, combined with refreshing 15 meter circles in the true lead at the center line).

4. To ride without stirrups for about 20 minutes each day in canter.

The Most Common Mistakes

1. Looking down, as if hoping to find the flying change on the ground!

2. Difficulty in shifting his weight aids from one side to the other side of the horse's back, usually because the rider is looking down!

3. Being too aggressive and surprising with the leg aids!

4. Standing in the stirrups!

My Recommendations

1. Train the flying changes without stirrups. There is no rider in the world that I've ever met who doesn't try to protect his bottom!

2. Carry the whip in the inside hand.

3. Give the aids for the flying change very clearly and carefully so the horse is able to translate them.

4. Give the aids through three strides, described here as a flying change from the right lead to the left lead. After successful half halts:

At the first stride, the rider encourages the horse's forward-ness through increased influence with the outside (left) leg and through a little bit stronger contact on the outside (left) rein.

At the second stride, the rider — keeping his eyes at the focal point at the horizon—moves his aids in position for the new lead side. The right leg is close behind the girth. The left leg is forward at the girth, the rider also still keeping a good contact on the left rein.

At the third stride, the rider — still keeping his eyes at the focal point — gives the signal for the change with the lower left leg and "parries," or restrains, the right rein (the new outside). *At the same moment,* the rider moves his weight from right to left (the right seat bone to the middle of the saddle). The left rein (the new inside) is released and allows the horse to move the left front leg forward.

5. When beginning to train the flying changes, make only one or two successful flying changes in both directions each day to avoid anticipation by the horse or unnecessary stress.

6. In the beginning, train the flying changes at the same location every day. When the horse starts to anticipate, it is time to chose a new location.

7. Make a halt as soon as possible after every attempt — successful or not—and reward the horse, getting him relaxed before the next attempt. *Create confidence!* This confidence is important for the quality of the single flying change and, later on, even more important for the execution of the different tempi changes.

THIRD LEVEL PATTERN 3
Flying Change of Lead

#1 IN THE SEQUENCE

PURPOSE
To perform a single flying change of lead in a corner of the arena.

Explanation
Proceed in trot at **M** on the left rein. After the corner by **H**, strike off in the right lead counter-canter. In the deep corner at **K**, perform the flying change.

Prepare to make a halt between **F** and **B**. At the halt, reward the horse and get him relaxed. After the halt, proceed in trot and perhaps repeat the pattern.

Observe
That the rider executes this training pattern without stirrups.

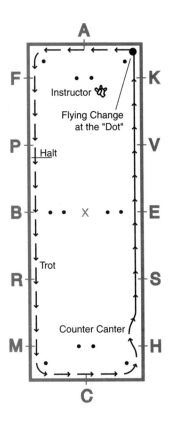

That the rider avoids making the usual mistakes as identified in **Third Level, Pattern 3**.

That the chosen location for the flying change — the deep corner— puts the horse in a situation where it is very natural for him to change the lead. In this pattern the horse has one wall on his right side and one wall in front of him.

That the rider gives the aids for the flying change through three strides in order to be very clear and translatable to the horse. Again, review **Third Level, Pattern 3.**

That the rider carries his whip in his inside hand, the right, in this case.

That if the horse is lazy or in previous attempts has been late behind, the rider, with sensitivity, uses his whip at the horse's flank at the third stride as a reminder.

THIRD LEVEL PATTERN 4
The Flying Change

#2 IN THE SEQUENCE

PURPOSE
To perform the flying change after a circle in the true lead, switching to another circle in counter-canter.

Explanation
Review **Second Level, Pattern 14.**

At **H**, begin the right lead counter-canter. At **E**, enter a quarter of the center 20 meter circle.

At the center line, ride a refreshing 15 meter circle right in the true lead. Returning to the center line, follow the center circle in counter-canter and prepare for the flying change.

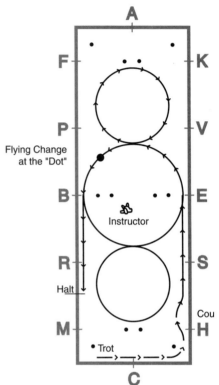

Flying Change at the "Dot"

Instructor

Halt

Trot

Cou

At the quarter line facing **B**, ride the flying change.
Prepare for a halt on the long side between **B** and **M**. After the halt, proceed in trot and perhaps repeat the pattern.

Observe
That the rider executes this training without stirrups.

That the rider avoids making the mistakes outlined in **Third Level, Pattern 3.**

That the chosen location for the flying change is a very natural situation for a flying change of lead. The horse makes the flying change from counter-canter to the true lead and in front of a wall, which works like an anvil, getting the horse to consider and translate the rider's aids.

That the rider, to be very clear and "translatable," gives the aids for the flying change through three strides. Again, review **Third Level, Pattern 3**.

That the rider carries his whip in his inner hand.

That if the horse is lazy or in previous attempts has been late behind, the rider, with sensitivity, uses his whip at the horse's flank at the third stride as a reminder.

THIRD LEVEL PATTERN 5
The Flying Change

#3 IN THE SEQUENCE

PURPOSE
To describe another appropriate location in the arena for a flying change of lead.

Explanation
Review **First Level, Pattern 6**

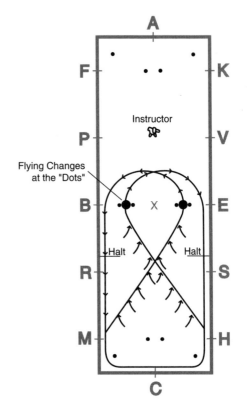

Flying Changes at the "Dots"

Begin at **C** in collected canter right lead. Ride half pass right between **M** and the gate of cones at the quarter line between **X** and **E**. Approaching the gate, prepare for a flying change of lead in between the cones. After the change, turn immediately left in to a 15 meter half-circle towards **B**. On the long side, prepare for a halt between **B** and **M**. After the halt proceed in collected canter left lead.

Ride half pass left between **H** and the gate of cones at the quarter line between **X** and **B**. Approaching the gate, prepare for a flying change of lead in between the cones. After the change, turn immediately right in to a 15 meter half circle towards.

On the long side prepare for a halt between "E" and "H". After the halt proceed in collected canter right lead and possibly repeat the pattern.

Observe

That the rider executes this training without stirrups.

That the rider avoids making the mistakes outlined in **Third Level, Pattern 3.**

That the rider, to be very clear and "translatable," gives the aids for the flying change through three strides. Again, review **Third Level, Pattern 3**.

That the rider carries his whip in his inner hand.

That if the horse is lazy or in previous attempts has been late behind, the rider, with sensitivity, uses his whip at the horse's flank at the third stride as a reminder.

That the rider imagines a small fence or a cavaletti between the two cones—a small fence which he is prepared to jump in combination with the flying change and the immediate turn.

THIRD LEVEL PATTERN 6
The Flying Change

#4 IN THE SEQUENCE

PURPOSE
To offer another appropriate location in the arena for the flying change of lead.

Explanation
At **C**, proceed in collected canter on the right lead towards **B**. At **B**, ride a 15 meter half-circle to the right and pass through the gate of cones at the quarter line between **X** and **E**.

Ride half pass right on the diagonal towards **M**. At **M**, go forward, prepare and ride the flying change of lead in the corner, where the horse is well framed by the walls. Compare with **Third Level, Pattern 4**. Prepare to halt on the short side of the arena at **C**.

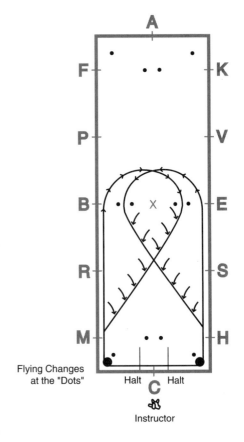

Flying Changes at the "Dots"

Halt   **C**   Halt

Instructor

At the halt, reward the horse and let him relax. After the halt, proceed in collected canter left lead towards **E** and repeat the half-circle left, the half pass left and the flying change of lead in the corner at **H**.

Prepare for the halt on the short side at C. After the halt proceed in collected canter right lead and repeat the pattern.

Observe
That the rider executes the training pattern without stirrups.

That the rider navigates and avoids the usual mistakes. See again **Third Level, Pattern 3.**

That the location chosen for the flying change is a very natural situation for a flying change of lead. The horse is well framed by the walls or fence.

That when approaching the corner at **M** or **H**, the rider thinks of how a ship docks at the pier in the harbor. However, try to keep the forehand off the track about 3 feet.

Comment
That thought or image can help the rider to understand how to prepare for a straight and clean flying change.

THIRD LEVEL PATTERN 7
The Flying Change

#5 IN THE SEQUENCE

PURPOSE

To introduce a new location in the arena for training the flying change of lead.

Explanation

Start at **H** in the left lead canter. At **E**, ride a 10 meter half-circle left. At **X**, canter down the center line. Prepare to make a flying change of lead to the right between **G** and **C**. After the flying change, prepare and make a halt on the long side between **M** and **B**, and reward the horse.

After the halt, either change rein and repeat the pattern from **H**, or begin again, this time on the right lead. At **B**, ride a 10 meter half-circle right and turn down the center line on the right lead. On the center line, prepare to make a flying change to the left between **G** and **C**.

After the flying change, prepare and make a halt on the long side between **H** and **E** and reward the horse.

Flying Change at the "Dot"

Instructor

Observe

That the rider executes this training without stirrups.

That the rider avoids making the mistakes outlined in **Third Level, Pattern 3.**

That the rider, to be very clear and "translatable," gives the aids for the flying change through three strides. Again, review **Third Level, Pattern 3**.

That the rider carries his whip in his inner hand.

That if the horse is lazy or in previous attempts has been late behind, the rider, with sensitivity, uses his whip at the horse's flank at the third stride as a reminder.

That the location chosen here for the flying change puts the horse in a situation without alternatives other than to change the lead, without running away.

THIRD LEVEL PATTERN 8
The Flying Change

#6 IN THE SEQUENCE

PURPOSE
To describe a new location in the arena for training flying changes.

Explanation
Ride the left lead canter from **M** to **H**. At **H**, prepare to turn left at S, passing around a cone.

Proceed towards **R** and perform a flying change to the right lead. After the change, go straight ahead and turn carefully around the cone. On the long side, make a halt and reward the horse.

Later, school the flying change from the right to the left lead between **P** and **V**.

Observe
That the rider *navigates.*

That the rider prepares his horse thoroughly for a flying change with half halts before the left turn at **S** around the cone.

That the rider approaching **R** imagines there is a cavaletti between the center line and **R**, and determines to approach and jump it.

That the rider avoids the four usual mistakes, when performing the flying change, as described in **Third Level, Pattern 3.**

That after the flying change the rider rides straight ahead and turns around the cone.

That if the horse is upset and tries to cut the turn, the rider decisively stops the horse in front of **R**.

Comment

If the rider is allowed (or is so instructed) to ride a three loop serpentine, the width of the arena, with flying changes of lead at the center line before solid training of this **Pattern 9,** the horse—smart as they are—will start to choose his own lines, to cut the turns and to run through the rider's hands without discipline.

I have trained many sensitive, nervous and hot horses, who need to be brought to a standstill in front of the wall. There they must be slowed down, calmed and relaxed before the exercise is repeated. *Create confidence!* With patience and repetition, they learn the lesson, making their flying changes with throughness and without stress.

Through the training of **Pattern 3** through **8** without stirrups, the rider should have developed the skill, sitting deeply in the saddle when schooling this **Pattern 9**. The rider should have the feeling of sitting *"in" the horse's back and not "on" his back.* It is necessary to have that feeling of sitting *in* the horse's back, before the rider is prepared, mature and skilled enough to begin the training of the tempi changes in the Fourth Level.

Tory Sawyer Photo courtesy of United States
Dressage Federation, Inc.

EXERCISES FOR FOURTH LEVEL

FOURTH LEVEL:
Increased Collection

---

*The movements are the counter changes
of hand in the half pass, the quarter- and half-
pirouettes in the canter, and the tempi changes
every fourth and third stride.*

FOURTH LEVEL PATTERN 1
Counter Change of Half Pass in Trot

AS IN AHSA FOURTH LEVEL,
TEST 3—"THE BOW TIE"

PURPOSE
To train the horse's obedience
and lateral flexibility and to
simplify the counter change
of half pass.

Explanation
Review **Second Level,
Pattern 11.**

Begin in trot at **V**. At **K**, ride a
10 meter half-circle left. From
D towards **E**, ride half pass left.
At **E**, ride a 10 meter circle
right. After the circle, half pass
right from **E** towards **G**. At **G**,
ride a 10 meter half-circle left.
Ride **H** to **E** to **K** in rising trot.

At **K**, repeat the pattern.

Variation #1: Train the pattern
in the opposite direction.

Variation #2: Train the pattern
in both directions, excluding the 10 meter circle at **E**.

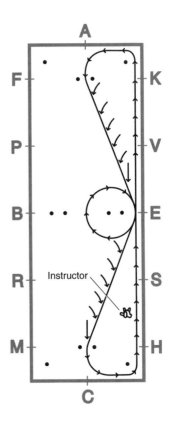

Observe
That the rider *navigates.*

That the rider allows the horse to enter the line from **D** to **E**
with good impulsion, before the aids for the half pass are
applied.

That the rider uses his inside leg (the hammer) effectively to
maintain the horse's contraction at the rib cage and to keep
him on the "line."

That the rider, upon approaching **E**, interrupts the half pass with some steps in leg-yielding, preparing the horse to enter the 10 meter circle right.

That the rider, after the circle, allows the horse onto the line **E** to **G** with good impulsion before the aids for the half pass are applied.

That the rider interrupts the half pass with some steps in leg-yielding, thus preparing the horse to perform the 10 meter half-circle left at **G**.

FOURTH LEVEL PATTERN 2
Counter Change of Half Pass in Trot

"THE SLALOM COURSE"

PURPOSE
To simplify the delicate problem of the counter change of half pass with a fun and amusing zig-zag exercise.

Explanation
Begin in collected trot at **V**. At **K**, begin a 15 meter half-circle left, and after passing outside the two cones around **D**, ride half pass left. The focal point is **E**. At the center line, begin leg-yielding away from the right leg and prepare to turn around the next cone.

At the same time, note the second focal point at **R**. After the turn, begin the half pass right. At the center line, begin leg-yielding and prepare to turn around the next cone.

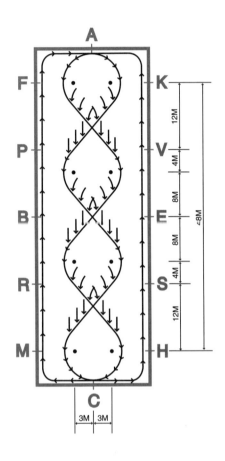

At the same time, note the third focal point, the arena corner. After the turn, begin half pass left. At the center line, begin leg-yielding from the right leg and prepare to turn around the next cone on a 15 meter half-circle right leading to the corner at **M**.

At **M**, follow the long side in rising trot to **F**. At **F**, begin a 15 meter half-circle right passing outside the two cones around **D** in collected, sitting trot. Repeat the pattern with the half pass right, but now with different focal points: the first **B**, the second **S**, and the third the arena corner.

Observe

That the rider looks at focal points *(navigates)* while turning his horse.

That the rider interrupts the half pass exactly at the center line and gives his horse the *opportunity* to be straight through the leg-yielding and *time* to make an elegant "stem" turn around the cone, forward into the next half pass.

That the rider, when he has learned the technique and attained the skill, should be able to ride the complete pattern without looking down at the horse for a single step.

Comment

Riders who are familiar with down hill skiing understand how to stem the rear end of the skis in order to change direction. In a similar way, on the horse the rider keeps the yielding outside leg behind the girth, increasing the use of it until the horse's rear end and body have been turned in the new direction.

Another analogy: the outside leg works like a tug, which is pushing a big ship at the stern and gets it to change direction.

Encourage the rider with comments such as: "Concentrate upon reaching **C** as elegant as possible," or "Dance with your horse," or "Look snobbish."

This exercise pattern can be used even at First Level for training leg-yielding.

At Second and Third Level, the exercise is useful when the aids for half pass have been introduced and when the horse and the rider are ready.

FOURTH LEVEL PATTERN 3
Counter Change of Half Pass in Trot

AS IN AHSA
FOURTH LEVEL, TEST 2

PURPOSE
To train this particular
movement, required in
Fourth Level.

Explanation
At **F**, proceed in collected
trot. At **K**, enter the diagonal
and ride half pass right.
The focal point is **M**. At **X**,
ride the counter change of
half pass.

At **X**, enter the diagonal from
X to **H** and ride half pass left.
The focal point is **H**.

Observe
That the rider carefully rides
through the corner at **K** and
allows the horse onto the
diagonal with good impulsion
before the aids for half pass
are applied.

That the rider navigates and that he and his horse both have
the same focal point, at **M**.

That the rider uses his inner (right) leg at the girth to keep
the horse on the line and to maintain the horse's bending
(contraction) at the rib cage.

That the rider, approaching **X**, interrupts the half pass with
some steps of leg-yielding away from the left leg to get the
horse straight and encourage him to move forward in the
new direction **X** to **H**.

That the rider, when he starts the leg-yielding, navigates using the new focal point **H**.

That the horse has the same focal point at H as the rider, before the aids for the new half pass left are applied.

Comment

Judges give one score for each performance of the half passes; the two half-passes are different movements in the test. Consequently, it is important for the rider to prepare the counter change of the half pass carefully, regaining any lost forwardness forward and impulsion before riding the second half pass **X** to **H**.

That the rider, when finishing the second half pass towards **H**, rides some steps in leg-yielding away from his right leg to get the horse straight and to encourage him to move forward through the corner at **H** with self-carriage.

FOURTH LEVEL PATTERN 4
The Half Pass in Canter

PURPOSE
To train the lateral work
in canter.

Explanation
Begin at **A** in the right lead
canter and ride half pass right **K**
to **X**. At **X**, ride a gait-refreshing
10 meter half-circle right and
follow the long side from **B** to **F**.
Repeat the pattern three times.

Completing the half pass right
the third time, ride a flying
change of lead at **X** and then,
immediately, a 10 meter half-
circle left towards **E**. Follow
the long side **E** to **K** and ride
the half pass left three times
between **F** and **X**.

Completing the half pass left
the third time, ride a flying
change of lead at **X** and then,
immediately, a 10 meter half-
circle right towards **B**.

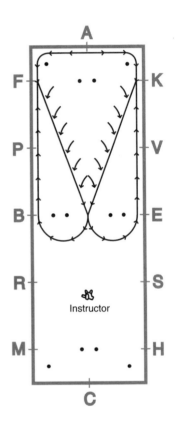

Observe
That the rider *navigates.*

That the rider comes onto the diagonal with good impulsion.

That the rider and the horse have the same focal point at **M**
and, respectively, at **H** before the aids for the half pass are
applied.

That the rider uses his inside leg actively at the girth.

That the rider, if the horse doesn't yield voluntarily or
collapses in the base of his neck, rides the horse with a

straight neck for a couple of strides in leg-yielding away from the outside leg, while at the same time decisively using the whip on the outside flank to remind the horse about discipline and order.

Comment

Riding this pattern the three times in the same direction as called for helps the rider and the horse understand the pattern and improve the performance while following the instructor's advice and suggestions.

FOURTH LEVEL PATTERN 5
The Canter Pirouette

PREPARATORY EXERCISE #1

PURPOSE
To create good confidence for the very collected canter on the spot.

Explanation
Begin with a 20 meter circle at **L** on the left lead. Each time the rider approaches the center line, he prepares to ride one or two strides of collected canter on the spot. After the attempt, the rider proceeds for a half of the circle for another attempt at the center line.

When the schooling attains a satisfactory result, the rider changes rein and begins to train on the right lead.

Observe
That the rider *creates confidence* in the horse, which means allowing an error and never punishing the horse.

That the rider, approaching the center line, keeps the same rhythm and tempo in the canter.

That the rider encourages the horse to bend the joints in his hind legs and to shift his weight back by using series of half halts.

That the rider uses the outside rein to decrease the speed, while the inner rein keeps the "axis" joint loose and the horse's mind relaxed.

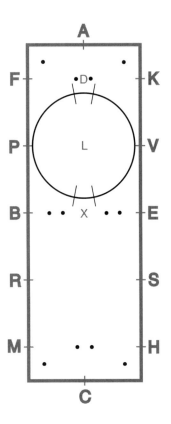

That as the speed over the ground diminishes, the energy and tempo must remain the same.

That the rider carries his whip in his outside hand, prepared to use it like a conductor's baton towards the horse's flank to keep the rhythm.

Comment

The rider should to imagine either that he is sitting on a rocking horse in a nursery, or that he is a truck driver dumping the load of sand from his dump truck. The rider should learn to gradually reduce the speed to zero MPH, while at the same time keeping the horse harmonious and confident.

FOURTH LEVEL PATTERN 6
The Canter Pirouette

PREPARATORY EXERCISE #2

PURPOSE
To create confidence for very collected canter on the spot and the transition down to a halt.

Explanation
Begin at **H** on the left lead canter. At **S**, make a soft quarter turn left and approach **R**. At the center line, begin a downward transition to a halt, riding the halt as close as possible to the wall at **R**.

After the halt, make a "box" turn left and repeat the exercise. (Review **First Level, Pattern 2**). When a satisfactory result is attained, begin the same training on the right lead at **M** via **R** towards **S**.

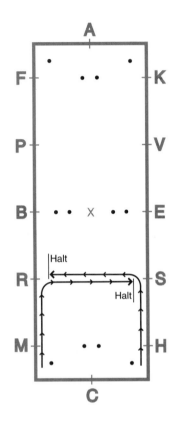

Observe
That the rider *creates confidence* for the increased collection, which means allowing a horse's error and avoiding punishing him.

That the rider, using series of half halts between the center line and the wall, gradually brings the horse to a stop very close to the wall.

Comment
Encourage the rider to imagine that he is parking a very expensive car in front of **S** or **R**, avoiding any kind of scratches.

Repetition is the mother of all good knowledge!

FOURTH LEVEL PATTERN 7
The Canter Pirouette

PREPARATORY EXERCISE #3

PURPOSE
To train the horse and the rider to make a quarter-pirouette in front of the wall.

Explanation
Strike off in collected canter either at **C** in left lead, or at **A** in the right lead. Make a soft turn left at **S** (or right at **V**) and approach the wall. The horse has previously trained to make a confident halt in front of **R** (or **P**). Review **Fourth Level, Pattern 6**.

When the horse, without any nervous reactions, begins the downward transition to a halt, the rider makes a "box" turn or a quarter turn on the haunches, which gives the quarter-pirouette to the left at **R**, or to the right at **P**.

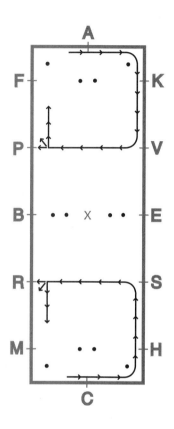

After the quarter-pirouette proceed in canter, make a halt, *reward the horse*, and perhaps prepare to repeat the exercise.

Observe
That the rider *navigates.*

That the rider keeps the canter all the way in to the wall.

That the rider prepares the "box" turn through some strides in the shoulder-fore left (right) position.

That the rider allows the pirouette to begin with his inside rein, opening his inside wrist.

That the rider uses his outside rein to control the turn stride by stride, and is prepared to counter lead with the rein, opening to the outside, if the horse anticipates the turn or throws his forehand, thus avoiding keeping the canter rhythm and the canter strides through the turn.

That the rider sits still to avoid using the forward driving aids too much, so as not to risk that the horse misunderstands the aids and tries to leave the pivot for the turn.

That the rider turns the horse with his weight aids and a yielding outside leg.

Comment
The wall works like an anvil in front of the horse and teaches him to turn on the spot, the pivot!

If the horse approaches the wall tense or nervous, anticipating the turn, just make the halt. The horse must approach relaxed and confident. *Don't punish!*

If the horse throws his forehand through the turn and ignores the outside counter leading rein, he is also showing no respect for the rider's inner leg. Make a halt. Don't punish, but make some turns on the forehand (review **First Level, Pattern 1**) to reestablish order and respect for the aids, especially the inner leg.

My Recommendation
Don't proceed with other pirouette exercises before this one works satisfactory.

The Most Common Mistakes
1. Looking down towards the inner side.

2. Collapsing at the inner waistline, so the weight aids work wrongly and contradict the aids for the turn.

3. Too strong a use of the forward pushing aids.

FOURTH LEVEL PATTERN 8
The Canter Pirouette

PREPARATORY EXERCISE #4

PURPOSE
This is a repetition of **Pattern 5**, adding a quarter-pirouette down the center line.

Explanation
Begin with a 20 meter circle at **L** on the left lead. Each time the rider approaches the center line, he prepares to ride one or two strides of collected canter on the spot (**Pattern 5**).

When the training attains a satisfactory result, the rider begins to make a quarter-pirouette left down the center line, followed by a halt at **L**. Later, the exercise is trained on the right lead.

Observe
That the rider *navigates* and focuses on the center line and **C** in order to be able to interrupt the pirouette in time!

That the rider prepares the quarter-pirouette with the aids for shoulder-fore left. This means that he displaces the horse's forehand to the outside with the inner leg, outside weight and counter leading outside rein until the forehand is about two feet outside the circle circumference and the hind legs have reached the center line (the pivot for the turn).

That the rider allows the quarter-pirouette by opening the inner leading wrist, moving his weight into the turn, and preparing to counter lead with the outside rein to control the canter strides and the rhythm of the turn.

That the rider *sits still*, which means he lifts his chin, keeps his chest erect, his waistline straight, and uses his lower legs carefully to avoid pushing the horse off the pivot.

Comment

If the horse approaches the center line nervous or tense, don't perform the quarter-pirouette. Instead, go back and train "the rocking on the spot" until it works well.

Don't punish! Create confidence! Spontaneous rewards!

FOURTH LEVEL PATTERN 9
The Canter Pirouette

PURPOSE
To train the working pirouette

Explanation
Start by riding the 20 meter circle around **L** on the left lead. Begin to spiral in to reach an 8 meter circle around **L**. On the 8 meter circle, increase the collection of the canter strides and perform one, two or three strides in travers left (haunches-in). Each attempt at the travers is released with a spiral out to the circumference of the 20 meter circle. Later, change the rein and lead, working from the other direction

When the rider and horse begin to improve, the number of strides in travers can be increased.

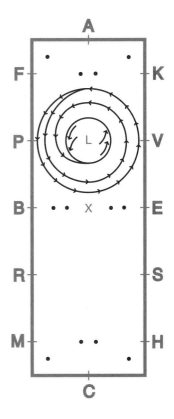

Observe
That the rider *navigates.*

That the horse observes the circumference of the circle while performing the travers.

That the rider thinks and acts rhythmically, as in half halt/travers/release/half halt/travers/release, and so on, getting the horse to shift his weight back and bending the joints in the hind legs. The horse should be trained to be confident, fit and able to "sit like a begging dog."

That the rider understands that this exercise is one way to

strengthen the horse's fitness and to increase the horse's confidence for the very slow tempo, stride by stride.

Comment

This exercise is demanding. Proceed carefully to avoid injuries in either the hocks or the stifles.

Through all the exercises suggested above on how to train pirouettes in canter, I have recommended that riders avoid making harsh corrections and, instead, suggested they strive to create confidence in the horse.

Horses are, however, smart and often the rider has to reestablish order. I would once again recommend using the turn on the forehand, which — sorry to say — is not included in the AHSA Training and First Level tests. The turn on the forehand gets the horse in front of the rider's legs, creating discipline for especially the inner leg and suppling the whole horse. Review **First Level, Pattern 1**, *"The Wash Sponge Exercise."*

FOURTH LEVEL. PATTERN 10
The Canter Pirouette

"THE TRIANGLE"
PREPARATORY EXERCISE #6

PURPOSE
To train the quarter-pirouette on the diagonal.

Explanation
Begin through the corner at **M** in the left lead canter. At **H**, enter the diagonal towards **B** and prepare to make a quarter-pirouette to the left at **I**.

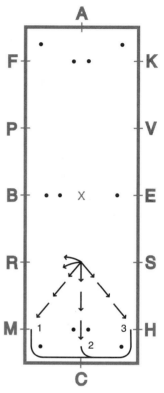

After the quarter-pirouette at **I**, follow the diagonal line from **I** towards the corner at **M** and perhaps repeat the quarter-pirouette. Later, begin in the corner at **H** and school the exercise in the opposite direction.

As shown on the drawing, the exercise starts with the quarter-pirouette at **I**. This is *Sequence A.* Then the exercise is developed to a third of a pirouette at **I**, down the center line towards **C**. This is *Sequence B.*

Lastly, the rider tries the half-pirouette back towards **H** on the diagonal. This is *Sequence C.*

My Advice
Proceed carefully and be prepared to go back to the basic exercises.

Observe
That the rider navigates for **I** immediately on the short side at **C**.

That the rider imagines a street man hole cover at **I**.

That the rider approaches the "man hole" in a very collected canter and rides left shoulder-fore, thus placing the forehand slightly to the right side of the man hole.

That the rider, when the inner left hind leg hits the man hole, navigates for the corner at **M**.

That the rider carefully reduces the horse's speed to almost "zero MPH" and allows him to perform the quarter-pirouette to the left.

FOURTH LEVEL PATTERN 11
The Canter Pirouette

PURPOSE
To train the half-pirouette on the diagonal but close to the wall. The wall works as the anvil in front of the horse as in previous exercises.

Explanation
Strike off in the left lead canter at **M**. Ride the diagonal from **H** to **B**. Close to **B**, when the horse responds the aids, perform the half-pirouette left and return towards **H**.

At **H**, make a flying change of lead to the right.

Observe
That the rider navigates and, when on the short side at **C**, imagines the point close to **B**, where he plans to ride the half-pirouette. Remember the imagery of the man hole cover in a street with a diameter of about 3 feet.

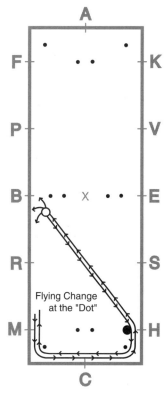

Flying Change at the "Dot"

That the rider, when approaching **B**, gradually reduces the speed to almost zero MPH through the use of many half halts.

That the rider, before he allows the horse to start the pirouette, displaces the horse's forehand to the right with some strides in shoulder-fore left in order to get the horse's inner hind leg well-centered for the turn.

That the rider, when the horse reacts to the wall (the anvil) remains calm and "cool," sits still and *allows* the horse to perform the half-pirouette in 3 or 4 strides.

That the rider throughout the half-pirouette *navigates* for **H** and is prepared to end the movement in time to be able to return towards **H** on a straight line for the flying change of lead.

Comment

If the horse is tense or tries to anticipate the half-pirouette, make a halt. Get the horse relaxed again. Then strike off in the left lead and make a new attempt.

Remember, *create confidence!*

FOURTH LEVEL PATTERN 12
The Half-Pirouette

AS IN THE AHSA
FOURTH LEVEL TESTS

PURPOSE
To train the half-pirouette on
the diagonal between **H** and **X**,
or **M** and **X**.

Observe
That the rider navigates, and
on the short side at **C**, imagines
the exact point on the diagonal
where he plans to ride the
half-pirouette.

That the rider displaces the
horse's forehand to the right side
of the "man hole cover" with a
few strides of shoulder-fore left.

That the rider approaching
the man hole gradually reduces
the speed almost to zero MPH.

That the rider, before allowing
the horse to begin the half-
pirouette, gets the horse's left
hind leg on the man hole cover.

That the rider, when allowing the horse to begin the half-
pirouette, is calm and cool and lets the horse do his job.

That the rider, while the horse turns, navigates for **H**, ready
to end the half-pirouette in time, like the *prima ballerina*
turns her head to a new focal point, before she executes one
or more pirouettes.

Comment
The chosen location for the man hole cover on the drawing is
closer to **X** than to **H**. Aesthetically, it probably is nicer to

make the half-pirouette exactly half way between **X** and **H**.

Previously, the flying change of lead at **H** was included in the movement, and many riders didn't ride the flying change carefully. Since 1996, though, the tests have identified the half-pirouette as one movement and the flying change is a separate one.

For less experienced riders and riders with inexperienced horses, the chosen location in this pattern allows more room and time after the pirouette for the rider to properly prepare his horse for a successful flying change.

In training sessions, the 'man hole' should often be marked in the footing. The instructor only needs to draw it with the heel of his boot, and it is a very good help for the rider to train for competition.

FOURTH LEVEL PATTERN 13
Flying Changes in Sequence

TEMPI CHANGES

PURPOSE
To introduce the flying changes of lead every eighth and sixth stride.

Explanation
Begin to train along the track on the long sides of the school and later on either the diagonals or the quarter lines.

Observe
That the horse is able to perform the single flying change calmly, straight and at an exact spot before the training of sequence changes starts. Review **Third Level, Pattern 9**.

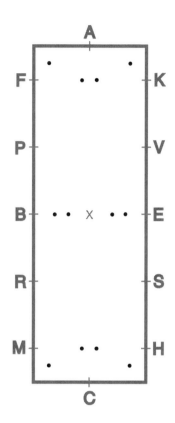

That the number of strides asked for between the changes depends on the horse's degree of training and sensitivity.

That the horse should be straightened before and after every change with the new outside rein.

That the horse, before and during every change, thinks *forward*.

That the rider's seat stays quiet and deep in the saddle before and during every change.

That the horse is *never* corrected harshly.

That if the horse starts to get nervous or tense, the rider rides some different movements in a different place and doesn't school the sequence changes for a few days.

Comment

The horse's confidence must be built up with more strides in between the changes.

The many halts used during the training of the single flying change have created a lot of confidence in the horse and a willingness to "wait." Now while learning flying changes in sequence, after each individual change, he anticipates a halt and a reward rather than expecting to run off. This mindset in the horse allows the rider to send the horse *forward* to each change rather than defensively trying to manage a tense horse with restrictive hands.

FOURTH LEVEL PATTERN 14
Flying Changes in Sequence

THE TEMPI CHANGES

PURPOSE
To train the flying changes of lead every fourth and third stride.

Explanation
Start at **R** in the left lead canter and prepare to ride the flying change of lead every fourth stride three times on the diagonal **H** to **F**.

Observe
That every time the rider strikes off in the canter, he decides beforehand the number of times he will change the lead and how many strides he will ride between the changes.

That the rider *navigates* and finds his focal point at **F**, and looks at it when he rides the diagonal.

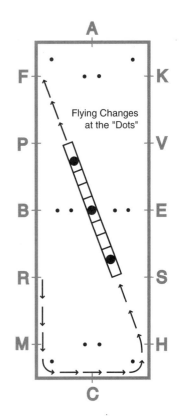

Flying Changes at the "Dots"

That the rider imagines the diagonal to be a very narrow street, with a width of about 3 feet.

That the rider prepares to follow the right side of the street when he — before the first flying change — enters the diagonal.

That the rider prepares the first flying change from left to right by yielding his straight horse to the left side of the street, and performing the first flying change to the right.

That the rider, at the first change, starts to count: "a - one; a - two; a - three; and — change." When the horse proceeds in the new lead, the rider discretely yields the horse to the right side of the street and rides the second flying change.

That the rider, at the second change, starts to count: "a - one; a - two; a -three; and — change." When the horse proceeds in the new lead, the rider discretely yields the horse to the left side of the "street" and rides the third flying change.

Comment

The ways of counting the strides between flying changes are very different among riders. My suggestion above helps the rider to count in rhythm with the strides.

The imagery of riding in a narrow street and discretely yielding the cantering horse from one side of the street to the other is a very good help in the beginning of this training. Yielding him into the support of the (soon to be) new outside leg prepares him to accept its influence for the change.

The rider is active with the outside leg.

The horse is engaged by the rider's weight and legs, and prepared to accept the aids for the flying change.

As the rider keeps his eyes at the focal point **F**, he still rides straight ahead even though he yields the horse invisibly.

Claes Dahlberg Photo courtesy of United States
Dressage Federation, Inc.

EXERCISES FOR FIFTH LEVEL

FIFTH LEVEL:
The Highest Degree of Collection

The movements are sequence flying changes of lead every second stride, the full pirouette in canter, piaffe and passage.

FIFTH LEVEL PATTERN 1
Flying Changes in Sequence

PURPOSE
Advice for the training of the flying changes of lead every second stride, "the two's."

Explanation
When the schooling of the flying changes of lead every 8th, 6th, 4th and 3rd stride begins to work well, it is time to begin with every second and, shortly, every stride, "the ones."

If the tempi changes don't work satisfactory, it preferable to ride some different movements in a another gait and not repeat the sequences for a few days.

It is also advisable to repeat **Third Level, Pattern 9**, training the single flying change to perfection!

My Recommendations
In most sports, the ability to concentrate is most important for a successful athlete. On the shooting range, this is very obvious: aim at the target — hit the target. Good concentration is 95% of a good result when shooting with a gun.

When the rider trains the sequences of flying changes, he must concentrate to navigate and to aim at the focal point; to avoid looking down and or twisting his hips or moving his upper body from side to side; to avoid joggling around, moving the legs too much; and to avoid changing the horse's flexing with too great exaggeration.

It is the instructor's duty to maintain a strict discipline about the matters described above!

If the rider concentrates enough, he can give accurate and nearly unnoticeable aids, and the horse stays *calm — forward — straight.*

Begin the training of the "two's" with only two changes first. Later, train three of them and gradually increase the number until the rider and the horse are able to perform five of the two's.

The flying change of lead every second stride is a very rhythmical movement. Before he strikes off, the rider must decide how many changes he intends to perform each sequence. Otherwise, he permits the horse to make the decisions, or just goes on until he or the horse makes an error.

The ways of counting the sequences is very different among riders. These is my suggestion to count for seven changes every second stride, or seven of "the two's:"

"a one - a two; a two - a two; a three - a two; a four - a two; a five - a two; a six - a two; a seven - a two."

The rider is able to count in rhythm with the canter and to give rhythmical aids, always knowing how many changes are performed, and performing the correct number of changes.

> "To our disgrace we must admit,
> that the desire for the beautiful in this fine art has
>
> decreased a great deal in our time, instead of,
> as was formerly the case, striving to gain the
>
> most difficult movements which constitute
> the grace of the manege and shed lustre on
>
> reviews, one nowadays contents oneself with to
> careless practice."
>
> —Robichon de la Guérinière,
> from *Ecole de Cavalerie*

FIFTH LEVEL PATTERN 2
Flying Changes in Sequence

PURPOSE
Advice for the training of the flying changes of lead every stride, that is, the single tempi or the "one's."

The Training Progression of the Rider
The best way for a rider to learn to perform the flying changes of lead every stride is to ride a schooled, skilled and *forgiving* old horse.

The rider must learn — without stirrups — to always give his aids in advance. If he, for instance, is to make flying changes from the left to right lead and back again to the left lead, he must apply the aids for the change back to the left lead as soon as he has given the aids for the first change (from left to right).

He must be one stride in advance; two of the one's is performed!

The rider must ride many, many "two's of the one's" from either the left lead or the right lead, and do them sitting with unexceptionable manners before he proceeds to make more than two of the one's. It is like climbing a ladder, learning step by step until the rider reaches fives of the one's in sequence.

At every training session, the instructor or the rider must decide how many tempi changes are to be performed. The rider must concentrate and learn to count while still keeping the horse on the aids. The counting part is easy: 1, 2, 3, and so on.

As this stage of training is very exciting, the rider often too early and too soon tries to ride 15 of the one's," like competitors on AHSA, Fifth Level, Test 4 presently requires.

If a less experienced rider, especially on an inexperienced horse, tries to perform too many of the one's too quickly, he can ruin the horse's confidence for the changes every stride. He will usually give the aids too late or unrhythmically, so the horse cannot translate them.

It is much better to train for five of the one's and, after a break, repeat five of the one's, a new break, and then five of the one's more and so on!

The length of the interruption in the break depends on the horse's reactions. The rider must wait for the next sequence until the horse, through using many half halts, is rebalanced, calm, forward and straight.

Often a rider must go back and re-school two of the one's to reestablish feeling for the rhythm and to carefully build sequences in harmony with the horse.

At each stride, the outside rein restrains the horse while the inside rein allows the stride. These alternate rein aids must rhythmically follow with every stride.

On very sensitive, nervous and hot horses, who by nature are very much forward, I suggest that the rider increase rhythmical influence with the outside restraining rein, and very carefully decrease the influence of the weight and leg aids.

The Training Progression of the Horse

When the horse has learned the flying changes every second stride, it is time to start the flying changes every stride, the tempi changes, or "the one's."

Technically, it is a question of teaching the horse a new gait. As far as my experience goes, I like to proceed very carefully throughout a whole year. Through that year, the goal is to build up the horse's confidence and skill to perform five of the one's *calm, forward and straight.*

The first and second month, the horse learns two of the one's, like left lead — right lead — left lead, or right lead — left lead — right lead. The rider should ride without stirrups and with strict self discipline for a correct seat and aids. Every time the horse responds calm, forward and straight, the rider should halt and reward the horse.

Throughout the first two months, the rider trains with a break between the two of the one's starting either from the left or the right lead. Again, the length of the break depends on the horse's reactions. Before each attempt the horse must, through the use of many half halts be calm, forward and straight. The rider must train the horse to stay on the aids and, without tension, repeat the sequence of two of the one's, time after time.

By the third month, the horse probably will be ready to learn three of the one's. If the horse makes a mistake or cannot translate the rider's aids, the rider must patiently repeat the two of the one's sequence until he has the feeling of sitting "in" the horse's back through the changes and then try again. The rider should never react harshly!

Most of the time, the errors are caused by the aids being given unrhythmically or too late. Review once again **Third Level, Pattern 9.**

By the end of the third month, the horse normally is able to take a break between the three of the one's and to stay calm, forward and straight. If not, the rider must repeat the basics! When the horse is learning a new gait, he needs time!

During the fourth month, the horse learns three of the one's, and four of the one's. If the basic training through the first three month has been successful, it shouldn't create any major problems. However, the step from two or three of the one's to, especially, four of the one's is a big one. The rider must be very patient. You can never punish a student (the horse) to understand or improve! Repetition is the mother of all good knowledge!

Training during the fourth month now includes sequences of different tempi changes with different length of interruptions like two of the one's, three or four times, or three of the one's, or two of the one's, three or four times, or four of the one's. It's like a drill to get the horse confident and listening to the aids, with submission. Again, it's a matter of teaching the horse a new gait and it takes time. *Festina lente* (Hurry slowly!)

During the fifth month, the horse is probably ready start to learn the sequence of five of the one's. It is, as I said in the introduction, the goal for a full year. That is true, but now through the fifth and following months, the horse must be schooled through a lot of combinations, which will keep him alert to the aids and prohibits every tendency of anticipation.

The rider always must decide in advance the number of strides of the one's he plans to ride. If not, he starts without concentration and goes on until either he or the horse makes an error. An error, which can create disappointment in the rider and despair in the horse for a long period of time. It is enough to reach five of the one's.

When the horse performs five of the one's with impulsion and elasticity, while calm, forward and straight by the end of the first year, it is no problem to increase the number of strides to seven of the one's as in the present AHSA Fifth Level, Test 3, or to 15 of the one's as in AHSA Fifth Level, Test 4.

The horse should trust his rider, and after five of the one's should seem to be asking the rider if he would like to perform some more strides of the one's, instead of nervously increasing the speed, falling on the forehand, and trying to pull the rider out of the saddle.

The rider must always remember that
repetition is the good mother of all knowledge!

FIFTH LEVEL PATTERN 3
The Full Pirouette in Canter

PURPOSE

Advice for the training of the full pirouette in canter.

From the exercises from **Fourth Level, Patterns 5** through **11**, the horse and rider have learned how to train the quarter- and half-pirouette in canter. If the rider and horse can successfully perform the half-pirouette, the execution of the full pirouette should not cause any major problem.

As the work of the full pirouette is a very hard strain for the horse, *it shouldn't be trained too often*. Even with horses who seem to be physically well able to perform the full canter pirouette, the rider must ride it sparingly.

The training is better directed to the repetition of the basic exercises to increase the horse's fitness, strength, confidence and the ability to transfer his weight to the inside hind leg.

The number of strides for a full pirouette varies from six to eight strides.

In a full pirouette, the rider must control the horse's attention, especially at the third stride, when the horse likes to anticipate and interrupt the pirouette as he is used to doing in a half-pirouette. The horse breaks the harmony of the foot-fall, jumps forward with his inner hind leg, and resists the rein influence, often over the bit and showing his underneck.

The rider must also control the horse's attention, again, especially at the third stride, and be prepared with a counter leading outside rein to prohibit the horse from throwing his forehand to the inside.

Sometimes I use a naive analogy to get the students to ride a full pirouette stride by stride, and to not just let it happen. Imagine that the horse is supposed to "cut like a knife a birth-day cake into six, seven, or eight pieces. The horse is in the middle of the cake with the hind legs on the 'man hole.'

Conducted by the rider, the horse elevates his forehand (accepts the half halt), turns his forehand, and descends his forehand and cuts a piece of the cake six, seven, or eight times.

This analogy has helped many students ride more distinctly and decisively, and to be fully aware of every stride throughout the pirouette.

FIFTH LEVEL PATTERN 4
The Piaffe

PURPOSE
Advice on how to train the piaffe.

The Training Progression of the Rider
The most common rider errors when riding the piaffe are tension, stiffness, very obvious aids applied at the wrong moment, upper body moving, and the hands unsteady and pulling backwards.

This means that the rider must train his seat and position to be well balanced to ride a correct piaffe. He must apply his aids with *feel* to enhance the horse's balance and rhythm.

The best way for a rider to learn to ride the piaffe is to ride a schooled, skilled and *forgiving* old horse. At first, the instructor can teach the student, without reins, on a horse doing piaffe in hand.

When I teach my students about the piaffe, I like to talk about *initial aids* and *supporting* aids. The piaffe can start from the halt, from the collected walk, or from the passage. As far as my experience goes, it is easier for the rider to apply correct aids in the walk. It is also easier for the horse to translate the aids as he moves forward, is in front of the rider's legs, and is ready to accept the aids for the half halts.

With series of half halts, the rider gets the horse to collect the walk, to get the horse to lower the quarters and bend the joints in the hind legs in order to begin the piaffe. Through the half halts, the rider uses his legs towards the horse's flanks (the position for collection). The schooled horse begins to translate these initial aids and to perform the piaffe. The horse immediately needs a spontaneous reward. He needs a receipt, that he correctly has understood the aids correctly!

It is now that he needs the supporting aids, which means that the rider moves his legs forward and closer to the girth (the forward pushing position).

The supporting aids usually get the horse to act more energetically and to elevate his forehand.

The horse must be encouraged to perform the piaffe with a *desire* to move forward. However, he is not supposed to move forward — he is supposed to perform nearly on the spot and give the judges and spectators *an impression of moving forward.*

When the horse performs the piaffe, the rider must be prepared with the initial aids to recollect him if he starts to be slow behind, as well as reward him with the supporting aids when he responds. The rider has to "play his instrument!"

With this mixture of initial and supporting aids, the rider is able to control the horse's rhythm and balance.

Too often, you see nervous, forward-leaning riders tapping and kicking the horses at the flanks. In that situation, the horses usually dutifully lift and bend their hind legs, but with high quarters and unrhythmically. The horse falls forward over his forehand with insufficient lifting of the front legs, which hardly leave the ground.

In the beginning of the rider's training, it is enough to do a few steps. Later, train to proceed and repeat a few steps of piaffe until the rider understands how to get the piaffe started and rewarded.

The work in piaffe and especially in passage is hard work for a horse! The very same hard work as when human athletes are drilled to make the "knee's up!" It is easy to create painful lactic acid with too much hard work. Therefore, *don't work the piaffe for too long and never use force.*

The whip should be considered to be similar to the music conductor's baton. It must be used, *not with force*, but sensitively and rhythmically close behind the rider's leg to *encourage* the horse!

The Training Progression of the Horse
Today's breeding brings a lot of horses talented for dressage. Of course, they each have different conformation and temperament, but many have in their genes the talent for the high school movements piaffe and passage.

Through the first and second year of basic training of the horse, you can sometimes invite him to increased collection, briefly demanding more activity from the hind legs while your weight and parrying hands keep the front end from hurrying away. Most of the time, he innocently and without problems responds with "double steps," a few extra-engaged, extra-shortened trot steps, not yet "on the spot." The rider understands that the horse has translated the aids for collection. When feeling the "double steps," the rider can look forward to the moment, when the horse will be physically and mentally prepared to develop them into actual piaffe steps.

"There is more than one way leading to Rome".

One way to train the piaffe is to work the collection in hand. It is a difficult task but pleasant, which must be introduced to the horse little by little. He must be trained to respect the restraining rein and the bit. He must be introduced to the whip all over his body and learn that the use of the whip is not supposed to be a punishment, but one way to explain to him how to act in the piaffe. It is pleasant to be on the ground and have an opportunity to observe the horse when he works. It is also an advantage for the horse to learn about the piaffe in hand without the problem of carrying the rider's weight.

A second way is to train the horse with the long reins. It is also a pleasant way to train a horse on the ground. However, it takes some time to learn to handle the horse with the long reins in order to achieve good communication and cooperation. The horse must be confident with the ground person at the reins with a whip in his hand and not be afraid or feel threatened.

In the walk on the track along the wall, let the horse take some steps in a slow very collected trot and begin to ask for some "double steps." If he responds, make a halt and praise him. If he doesn't understand, a sensitive horse sometimes tries to escape or to kick towards the rider. Be patient! Don't punish harshly! Go on, little by little, a couple of times a week and he will learn the piaffe.

Repetition is the mother of good knowledge!

A third way to train the piaffe is to use the horse's desire to return to his stable during trail rides, especially about 11.30

a.m., when he knows his crib is filled with grain! I have trained this way with many horses. I have chosen about four spots on my way home where I give the aids for "double steps." Every trail ride, I return to the same spots, and sooner or later the horses have started the piaffe for the initial aids. And they have performed with a real desire to move forward. My problem using this method has been to keep them as straight as possible and to try to relax them.

The more common way is to train along the wall. From the collected walk, the horse is allowed to take one or two steps in a very collected trot. Then the rider gives the initial aids for piaffe. The poll should be the highest point of the neck. *Do it little by little!* As soon as the horse responds, the rider gives the horse a spontaneous reward, when he changes to give the horse the supporting aids to encourage the horse's desire to move forward. The supporting aids also increase the horse's activity both at the shoulder and elbow joints.

When the horse starts to respond with the double steps in the walk, the rider proceeds in collected trot and performs shoulder-in along the wall. Slowly the rider moves the forehand in front of the rear end and begins with the outside rein to collect the horse into some piaffe steps. After some attempts, the horse starts to understand and performs a nice piaffe because his inner hind leg has been bent and has come in under his center of gravity to lighten the horse's forehand.

The rider can imagine that he is sitting on a scale with two bowls, one in front of him and one behind him. The initial aids as well as the aids for half halts means to the horse that he is to lower his quarters and to bend the joints in the hind legs, at least until a horizontal level is achieved.

When the horse responds to the initial aids, he has to be released at least to a horizontal level. If the horse starts to be behind the rider's legs and doesn't respond the supporting aids, the rider must decisively push him forward into a working trot or medium trot.

Sometimes a ground person— normally the instructor — can support the horse with the whip. *But it shouldn't happen too often.* The horse often reacts with tension. The footfall in the hind legs changes rhythm nervously. The horse starts to be tense in his neck. The front legs work without suppleness and with straight knees.

This tense situation can be caused by too hard demands too early in the training. The tense situation can cause the horse to start swaying his quarters from side to side, or trying to balance his forehand from side to side. This also can depend on his conformation; perhaps the angles in his hind legs don't allow the horse to "sit" like Lipizzaners or Andalusians in the classical way.

If the horse learns these bad habits, it is very difficult or even impossible to get rid of them. In the Grand Prix de Dressage, the rider isn't allowed to carry a whip. This is why the rider, in my opinion, must train the horse in piaffe for only short periods, and during the training keep the horse straight, supple and *willing*.

As said above, the piaffe should be performed in the classical way. The horse's conformation sometimes complicates that. Then the rider should be happy if the horse willingly, relaxed and supplly makes the amount of required steps his way.

The famous German horse Rembrandt, ridden by Nicole Uphoff-Becker to victories at the Olympic Games and Championships always showed the correct amount of steps in piaffe *on the spot*, in flawless rhythm and made his transitions in and out of the piaffe with excellence.

But as Rembrandt's piaffe wasn't really classical (he didn't lower his quarters the classical way), his high scores caused a lot of debate between judges and trainers as well as owners and spectators.

FIFTH LEVEL PATTERN 5
The Passage

PURPOSE
Advice on training the passage.

The Training Progression of the Rider
Like the other highest movements, he best way to learn to
ride the passage is to ride a schooled, skilled and *forgiving*
old horse.

The most common errors are to miss the correct moment to
let the passage stride out forward, or to not follow the movement sufficiently, or not to sit quietly and avoid disturbing
the horse's balance.

When the rider prepares to pick up the passage from walk,
he carefully begins to collect the walk with the *initial aids* (the
same aids used to initiate the piaffe). When the horse reacts,
the rider gives him *supporting forward driving aids* and
prepares the horse to stride out *forward*.

The preparation is intended to make the horse carry his head
and neck a little deeper and rounder to avoid him collapsing
in his back when he strides out.

The author riding Eko at Stockholm, 1972. Claes Dahlberg Photo courtesy
of United States Dressage Federation, Inc.

When the horse moves out in the strides of passage, the rider experiences a real highlight of riding. As in all other parts of riding, however, he must support with half halts, rebalancing or recollecting the horse to avoid him dropping his back or starting to get tense in the back and neck muscles.

The Training Progression of the Horse

The passage is a very natural movement for the horse. He has often performed the passage, either because he has been surprised or afraid of something, or he has had a reason to show his pride and happiness.

When after all his training, he starts to be straight and has achieved a high degree of collection, it is time to introduce him to the passage.

As I suggested when training the piaffe, I recommend beginning during trail rides or in open fields. For most horses, it is easy to translate the rider's aids for the passage when they are given in the medium trot as a transition to passage.

What is not longer supposed to go forward is now supposed to change to an elevation into the passage.

In the beginning the rider should only look for a few strides.

A natural and common error is, sorry to say, trying to begin the passage with restraining reins, which is why the horse misunderstands the aids and the impulsion to stride out is lost.

FIFTH LEVEL PATTERN 6
The Passage

PURPOSE

To train the horse to pick up the passage on a 20 meter circle.

Explanation

Start at **P** on the left rein in collected trot. At **B**, begin to ride the 20 meter circle at **X** in medium trot.

At **E**, follow the 20 meter circle and apply the aids for passage. At **B**, ride a transition to the working trot rising. Follow the track and at **K**, perhaps repeat the pattern.

Later, change the rein and train on the other hand.

Observe

That at **B**, the rider begins the medium trot on the 20 meter half-circle from **B** to **E** with an inside suppleness in the horse's poll and inside rib cage, but in principle a straight horse.

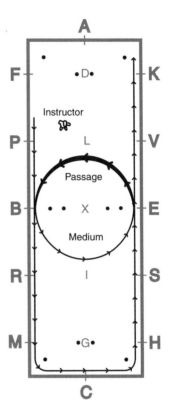

The rider is also advised to think of "banking" the horse like the pilot banks his aircraft in a turn, or the motorcycle driver banks his motorcycle when he turns into a curve. In both cases, the images remind the rider to focus the turning energy *inward* with a balance and support that works against the centrifugal force created by the added speed of the medium trot.

That at **E**, the rider—keeping the inside suppleness—carefully increases the contact on the outside rein and supports the strides out with a rhythmically working outside leg close to the girth.

Comment

The use of the outside leg is similar to the use of a drum stick towards the bass drum in a band, to create and to keep the rhythm.

That the rider, in the beginning, is prepared to release the horse as he translates the aids. *Proceed little by little.*

Later, change the rein and train on the right hand.

FIFTH LEVEL PATTERN 7
The Passage

AS FOUND IN AHSA
FIFTH LEVEL, TEST 3

PURPOSE
To prepare the required
movements with a more
simple exercise.

Explanation
Begin on the short side at **C**
in collected trot. At **H**, ride the
medium trot on the diagonal
towards **F**. At **F**, ride the
transition to passage.

At **A**, ride a transition to a
piaffe of 7 - 8 steps.

Observe
That at **F**, the rider, through
the transition from medium
trot to passage, doesn't begin
to restrain the horse with
the reins.

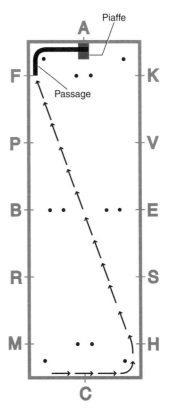

That the rider keeps the horse
basically straight through the
corner, except for a slight position to the right at the poll, with
respect for the inner right leg.

That through the corner the rider supports the strides out
with a rhythmically working outside leg close to the girth.
Review **Fifth Level, Pattern 6**.

Comment
It is easier for the horse to translate the aids for passage (and
for the rider to give them) through a corner than it is as
required in the test on the long side between **P** and **F**.

FIFTH LEVEL PATTERN 8
"The Hinge"

PURPOSE
To train the horse's flexibility
and submission.

Explanation
Begin at **B** on the right rein in
collected trot. Between **K** and **V**,
perform travers right.

At **V**, ride a transition to
shoulder-in right. Perform
shoulder-in right between
V and **E**.

At **E**, make a transition to renvers left. Perform renvers left
between **E** and **V**. At **S**, make a
transition to the right lead canter and turn immediately onto
the 20 meter half-circle at **S**.

At **R**, possibly repeat the
pattern.

Later, change the rein and train
the exercise from **F**.

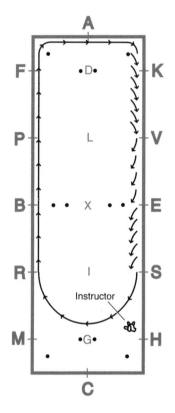

Observe
That during the travers, the horse looks *straight* down the
track.

That the rider performs the shoulder-in on the second track,
about five feet off the wall, so that the quarters continue on
the same line they began in the travers and do not deviate to
the outside.

That the rider keeps the horse's hind legs five feet off the wall
when riding the renvers, and the angle of the horse relative to
the track remaining the same as the horse reverses his bend
from shoulder-in to renvers.

That the rider gives the aids for the right lead collected canter *in combination* with the transition from renvers left to the right lead.

That the rider *navigates* and looks at the instructor down the long side.

Comment

This exercise improves the horse's flexibility and his submission as well as his suspension. It is an aerobic exercise. *It is fun to ride!* It keeps the rider busy every step and trains him to increase his skill to coordinate his aids.